100 TRAINS 100 YEARS

A CENTURY OF LOCOMOTIVES AND TRAINS

100 TRAINS 100 YEARS

A Century of Locomotives
and Trains

photography by

FREDRIC WINKOWSKI
FRANK D. SULLIVAN

text by Richard E. Mancini

additional photography by Ken Ganz

CASTLE BOOKS

This edition published in 2003 by

CASTLE BOOKS ®
A division of Book Sales, Inc.
114 Northfield Avenue
Edison, New Jersey 08837

Published by arrangement with
Frederic Winkowski Photo Publications
48 West 71st Street
New York, New York 10023

10 9 8 7 6 5 4 3 2

Library of Congress Cataloging-in-Publication Data is available.

ISBN-13: 978-0-7858-1669-0   Printed in China
ISBN-10: 0-7858-1669-0

CONTENTS

Introduction

The Decade 1900 – 1909

1900	Rio Grand Southern Railroad No. 20	12
1901	Central Railroad of New Jersey No. 592	14
1902	Chesapeake & Ohio Railway No. 377	14
1903	Illinois Central Railroad No. 790	16
1904	Philadelphia & Reading Railroad No. 1187	18
1905	New York, Chicago & St. Louis Railroad (Nickel Plate Road) No. 44	18
1906	Greenbrier, Cheat & Elk Railroad No. 1	21
1907	Delaware & Hudson Railway Gondola No. 8148	21
1908	GVB (Graz, Austria) No. 120	22
1909	Baltimore & Ohio Railroad No. 10	23

The Decade 1910 – 1919

1910	SNCF (French National Railways) "Little Yellow Train"	24
1911	Berlin Mills Railway No. 7	29
1912	Washington Terminal Company No. 500-501	29
1913	Maine Central Railroad No. 519	30
1914	Canadian National Railways No. 47	31
1915	Brooks-Scanlon Corporation No. 1	32
1916	Rahway Valley Railroad No. 15	32
1917	Canadian National Railways No. 3254	35
1918	Baltimore & Ohio Railroad No. 4500	36
1919	New Haven Trap Rock Company (Branford Steam Railroad) No. 43	36

The Decade 1920 – 1929

1920	Canadian National Railways No. 3377	38
1921	Lowville & Beaver River Railroad No. 1923	40
1922	Public Service Electric & Gas Company No. 6816	40
1923	Norwood & St. Lawrence Railroad No. 210	43
1924	Strasburg Railroad No. 90	46
1925	Grand Trunk Western Railroad No. 6039	51
1926	Central Railroad of New Jersey No. 1000	53
1927	E. J. Lavin & Company No. 3	53
1928	Baltimore & Ohio Railroad No. 5300 (President Washington)	54
1929	Baldwin Locomotive Works No. 26	55

The Decade 1930 – 1939

1930	Canadian Pacific Railway No. 2816	58
1931	Pennsylvania Railroad No. 6755	60
1932	Philadelphia & Western No. 205 (Bullet Car)	62
1933	Boston & Maine Railroad No. 3713	62
1934	Pennsylvania Railroad No. 4800	65
1935	Pennsylvania Railroad No. 5690	68
1936	Bullard Company No. 2	68
1937	Baltimore & Ohio Railroad No. 51	71
1938	Canadian Pacific Railway No. 2929	73
1939	Pennsylvania Power & Light Company No. 4094	73

The Decade 1940 – 1949

1940s	The War Years/Gatefold	74
1940	Union Pacific Railroad No. 4012	78
1941	Chesapeake & Ohio Railway No. 1604	81
1942	U.S. Army Corps of Engineers No. 8077	82
1943	Pullman Company No. 7437	83
1944	New York, Chicago & St. Louis Railroad (Nickel Plate Road) No. 757	85
1945	Pennsylvania Railroad No. 5901	85
1946	Chesapeake & Ohio Railway No. 490	87
1947	Reading Company No. 2124	89
1948	New York, New Haven & Hartford Railroad No. 0673	90
1949	Chesapeake & Ohio Railroad No. 1309	93

The Decade 1950 – 1959

1950	Reading Company No. 902	94
1951	Erie Railroad No. 835	96
1952	Western Maryland Railway No. 236	97
1953	Western Maryland Railway No. 195	99
1954	Remington Arms Company No. 2	100
1955	Baltimore & Ohio Railroad No. 633	100
1956	Florida East Coast Railway No. 663	102
1957	New York, New Haven & Hartford Railroad No. 140-141 (Roger Williams)	102
1958	New York, Chicago & St. Louis Railroad (Nickel Plate Road) No. 514	105
1959	Oakland Bay Rapid Transit No. 167	107

The Decade 1960 – 1969

1960	Metro-North Commuter Railroad No. 2024	108
1961	Baltimore & Ohio Railroad No. 1961 (Daylight Speedliner)	110
1962	Delaware & Hudson Railway No. 413	110
1963	New York Central Railroad No. 4096	112
1964	Baltimore & Ohio Railroad No. 7402	115
1965	Maine Central Railroad No. 228	115
1966	Baltimore & Ohio Railroad No. 3684	116
1967	Lackawanna Valley Railroad No. 901	116
1968	New York, Susquehanna & Western Railway No. 3000	118
1969	Monongohela Connecting Railroad No. 701	119

The Decade 1970 – 1979

1970	Conrail No. 6905 and No. 6908	120
1971	Conrail No. 7896	122
1972	Canadian Pacific Railway No. 5425	122
1973	Delaware & Hudson Railway No. 7418	124
1974	Reading & Northern Railroad No. 2399	124
1975	Stourbridge Railroad No. 44	127
1976	Florida East Coast Railway No. 501	129
1977	Boston & Maine Railroad No. 314	129
1978	Conrail No. 1983	129
1979	SNCF (French National Railways) TGV	131

The Decade 1980 – 1989

1980	Florida East Coast Railway No. 445	132
1981	New Jersey Transit No. 4129	134
1982	Amtrak No. 953	134
1983	Conrail No. 6702	136
1984	Conrail No. 6563	136
1985	Canadian Pacific Railway No. 3057	138
1986	Florida East Coast Railway No. 434	140
1987	Conrail No. 5024	141
1988	Tri-Rail No. 805	142
1989	Conrail No. 6042	142

The Decade 1990 – 2000

1990	Metro-North New Haven Line	144
1991	Conrail No. 6151	146
1992	Soo Line No. 6059	146
1993	Durango & Silverton Narrow-Gauge Railroad No. 480	148
1994	Canadian Pacific Railway No. 1828	148
1995	New Hope & Ivyland Railroad No. 1513	149
1996	Amtrak No. 700	152
1997	Conrail No. 4122	153
1998	Middletown & Hummelstown Railroad No. 1016	154
1999	Delaware-Lackawanna Railroad No. 310	154
2000	Amtrak Acela	156

The Next Century	158
Railroad Museums	162
Selected Operational Historic/Tourist Railroads	162
Photo Credits	163
Acknowledgments	164
Index	165

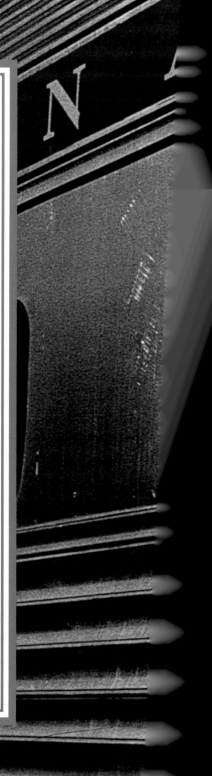

INTRODUCTION

Train. It's quite a potent little word—one that conjures up immediate images of power, movement, adventure, and excitement. And there are probably very few people on earth who can't instantly recognize the meaning of that word, in any language—or what the remarkable machine it describes has done for our society during the past 150 years.

Traveling at greater speeds and with less effort and expense has long been a preoccupation with the human animal—and never more so than in the industrialized culture of the nineteenth and twentieth centuries. Consider for a moment the number of ways in which this society has striven to go farther and faster over the last 100 years. Then think about the most efficient way we've found to move large amounts of our "stuff" and great numbers of ourselves overland at one time— and there's that word again: *train.*

Although railroading as we know it began in earnest during the first quarter of the nineteenth century, the last 100 years have witnessed quite a bit of history on the rails. And the trains that have come and gone during that time have played a crucial role in our nation—and in the lives of its people.

Now, standing on the brink of the twenty-first century—and a new millennium—we look back at every year of the previous century to discover 100 very special trains. Each of them has touched countless lives, and each has its own particular story to tell.

The Chronology

The authors have considered each year since 1900 and have selected a locomotive, trainset, piece of rolling stock, or other railroad equipment to represent it. In many cases the subject was built, purchased, or actually in service during that year. In others, it may have been connected with a significant historical event or trend, or it is an example of a type introduced at that time. We based our selections on a number of criteria, including historical significance, uniqueness, aesthetic qualities, technical innovations, availability, individual history, and visual excitement, as well as that special something that draws both veteran railfans and the casual observer to a particular locomotive or train.

Wherever possible, we've selected machines in operating condition and still in active service for passenger, freight, tourist railroads, or rail museums. Others are currently on static display at museums or historic sites. Many of the trains on these pages are the property of working railroads, while others are owned and maintained by the many fine museums and historical societies dedicated to preserving railroading's rich heritage.

The Trains

A process filled with constant discovery, the production of this book has enabled us to

become familiar with the seemingly infinite variety of equipment produced and operated by North American railroads during the twentieth century. Along with images of locomotives powered by steam, electric traction, diesel-electric motors, gas turbines and other propulsion methods, these pages also present an array of diverse rolling stock: self-propelled railcars, trainsets, interurbans, passenger coaches, sleeper cars, freight gondolas, tank engines, boxcars, yard switchers, wrecking cranes, and the list goes on.

A range of significant producers of twentieth-century railroad freight, passenger, and work equipment manufactured the trains featured in this book. The work of such firms as the American Locomotive Company (Alco), Baldwin, Lima, General Motors Electro-Motive Division, General Electric, Budd, Pullman-Standard, Montreal Locomotive Works/Bombardier, Alsthom, Morrison-Knudsen, H. K. Porter, J. G. Brill, and many others is represented here. We have striven to impart as much information about these builders and their individual models as availability and space would allow.

The Railroads

Finally, in showcasing the trains that helped shape the twentieth century, we have also attempted to introduce the reader to those storied institutions that made them possible: the railroads themselves, from vast national systems to tiny local "short lines." The lines represented in these pages include Union Pacific, New York Central, Pennsylvania Railroad, Nickel Plate Road, New Haven, Baltimore & Ohio, Canadian Pacific, Chesapeake & Ohio, Soo Line, Delaware-Lackawanna, FEC, Boston & Maine, Reading, Erie Railroad, Western Maryland, Lehigh Valley, Amtrak, Conrail, and many others.

A Century on Rails

Along with the Industrial Revolution, the first half of the nineteenth century had given birth to the railroads, and the second half had launched their "Golden Age." Throughout those years, the 4-4-0-type steam locomotive (employing four "pilot" wheels in front, four "driving" wheels, and no "trailing" wheels) became the dominant engine on American railroad tracks, with nearly 25,000 ultimately in use. Typified by *The General* of Civil War fame and emblematic of the "Old West," the configuration was so closely associated with U.S. railroads it was known simply as the "American Standard."

But as the nineteenth century wore on, the quest for greater locomotive power signaled the end of the 4-4-0's reign. By the time that enterprising era gave way to the twentieth century, a new generation of engineers, inventors, industrialists, and "railroad men" were striving to speed the transport of passengers and freight by rail—and earn bigger and bigger profits—by creating bigger and faster locomotives. Most still used steam power, but others employed versions of the internal-combustion engine, or electric motors, or combinations of the two. And, as you will see for yourself, the results of these efforts were, if not always successful, at least indelible proof that there really *is* "something about a train."

1900
Rio Grande Southern Railroad No. 20

Schenectady 4-6-0 (Ten-Wheeler)
Narrow-Gauge Steam Locomotive

By the 1880s, steam locomotives with the venerable eight-wheel 4-4-0, or "American Standard," arrangement (four pilot wheels, four driver wheels, no trailer wheels) were no longer up to the task of hauling the steadily increasing tonnage as America moved westward. The next two decades saw the rise of a more powerful alternative capable of supporting the larger boiler and firebox required to produce the desired horsepower: the 4-6-0, prosaically dubbed the "ten-wheeler," early versions of which had been produced since the 1860s.

Several other innovative ten-wheeled configurations would soon take to the rails, including the 4-4-2 (Atlantic), 2-8-0 (Consolidation), and 2-6-2 (Prairie) types. But the earliest viable arrangement (and perhaps the most obvious) was the 4-6-0, created by adding a third driven axle to the old 4-4-0 scheme. Approximately 16,000 of these locomotives were produced, and they pulled the lion's share of American express passenger trains between 1880 and the first two decades of the twentieth century.

The stately narrow-gauge ten-wheeler shown here was built by the Schenectady works in 1899 for service in the new century. As seen at the Colorado Railroad Museum at Golden, No. 20 sports the livery of the Rio Grande Southern, the famous narrow-gauge line that laboriously negotiated 162 miles of winding track through the Rocky Mountains between 1893 and the early 1950s.

1900-1909

Steam is king on the world's railroads as the "American Century" dawns full of promise. And just as they helped tame the Western frontier, "iron horses" built by Alco, Baldwin, and Lima blaze a trail for the nation's growing industrial power.

1902
Chesapeake & Ohio Railway No. 377

Baldwin 4-6-0 (Ten-Wheeler)
Steam Locomotive

Although classic ten-wheeler locomotives were soon rendered obsolete by new configurations and advancing technology, they continued to be built well into the new century. The example from Maryland's B&O Museum detailed here was originally manufactured in 1902 by Philadelphia's Baldwin Works as CC&L No. 103, later becoming No. 377 for the fabled Chesapeake & Ohio line.

Beginning life as the Louisa Railroad in 1836, and later the Virginia Central, the Chesapeake & Ohio acquired its new name after expanding westward to the Ohio River in the years following the Civil War. An important coal-hauling line linking the Atlantic seaboard with America's inland waterways, the "new" C&O was completed in 1873, expanded to Cincinnati in 1889, and modernized throughout the 1890s.

No. 377 began its service with C&O during a period of even greater expansion for the railway. Between 1890 and 1920, the line linked with coal branches in West Virginia and Kentucky, gained access to the Great Lakes through Ohio, and acquired a line from Cincinnati to Chicago. During the 1920s it joined the Nickel Plate Road and the Pere Marquette Railway as part of a large railroad empire. The C&O later survived the Depression and World War II to emerge as one of America's leading railroads and the world's largest hauler of bituminous coal. At its peak, the line had no less than 16 different wheel arrangements in service; No. 377 represents one of the earliest.

1901
Central Railroad of New Jersey No. 592

Alco 4-4-2 (Atlantic) Camelback
Steam Locomotive

As the nineteenth century drew to a close, American railroads strove to find more efficient methods of increasing locomotive power. A host of new steam-locomotive designs featuring ten or more wheels, introduced in the 1880s and the next few decades, were capable of more power than earlier 4-4-0 or even 4-6-0 engines. Among these was the 4-4-2 type, whose two additional trailing wheels supported a wider, deeper firebox, as well as a larger-capacity boiler—elements essential to greater horsepower.

Known as the "Atlantic" type ever since first appearing on the Virginia-to-Florida Atlantic Coast Line in

1893, the 4-4-2 became a fixture on passenger lines on the eastern seaboard. Later in the 1890s, 4-4-2 Atlantics—featuring wide fireboxes, pairs of compound cylinders, and separate camelback or Mother Hubbard cabs for the engineer—pulled fast trains from Philadelphia to New Jersey coastal resorts for the Atlantic City Railroad. These "Atlantic City Fliers," with running speeds of about 90 mph, were among the world's fastest scheduled trains at the time, and their success led the competing Pennsylvania Railroad to adopt camelback 4-4-2's for many of their routes as well.

No. 592, the splendid Atlantic camelback engine shown here, which was built in 1901 by the American Locomotive Company (Alco) Brooks Works, saw service with the Central Railroad of New Jersey. Today it resides at Baltimore's B&O Railroad Museum, delighting visitors who come to relive the glorious "Age of Steam."

1903
Illinois Central
Railroad No. 790

Alco 2-8-0 (Consolidation)
Steam Locomotive

Its restored boiler gleaming brightly, Illinois Central No. 790 stands proudly in the yard at Pennsylvania's Steamtown National Historic Site—a splendid reminder of the "Golden Age of Steam." The 2-8-0 Consolidation engine, built in 1903 at Alco's Cooke Works in New Jersey, first saw service as Chicago Union Transfer Railway No. 100, but was sold in 1904 to Illinois Central, which modernized it with a superheater in 1919.

Like most Consolidation-type engines, No. 790 (which was renumbered from No. 641 in 1943) pulled freight for most of its long career with the Illinois Central Railroad, whose main line stretched 912 miles from Chicago to New Orleans via Cairo, Illinois, at the turn of the century. All told, the Illinois Central System operated over 4200 miles of track at the time, and later expanded to over 6800 miles in 14 states. No. 790 most likely chugged along much of that mileage before finally ending regular service in the late fifties. A short time later, the old warhorse was pulled out of virtual retirement to help stranded diesel-electrics plow across flooded Iowa tracks, a feat which it repeated in 1965—once again attesting to the great power of steam.

1903

1905
New York, Chicago & St. Louis Railroad (Nickel Plate Road) No. 44

Alco 4-6-0 (Ten-Wheeler)
Steam Locomotive

In December 1905, Alco's Brooks Works in Dunkirk, New York, delivered ten brand-new 4-6-0's (numbered 40 through 49) to the New York, Chicago & St. Louis Railroad, later known as the "Nickel Plate Road." One of those ten-wheelers, No. 44, is shown here at Scranton, Pennsylvia's Steamtown National Historic Site.

The New York, Chicago & St. Louis Railway began operation in 1882 and emerged from bankruptcy in 1887 as the New York, Chicago & St. Louis *Railroad*. By 1900 the line operated just over 500 miles of track between Chicago and Buffalo, and eventually became part of the vast New York Central System.

When No. 44 began its service with the N.Y., C. & St.L., those letters were emblazoned on its tender, which held 14 tons of coal and 5,500 gallons of water in its tank. Only after the line picked up its now-familiar nickname, and after this locomotive was renumbered as No. 304 in 1910, did it carry the logo of the Nickel Plate Road. Later in its long career, this workhorse also ran for both the Akron, Canton & Youngstown and the Dansville & Mount Morris Railroads.

1904
Philadelphia & Reading Railroad No. 1187

Burnham, Williams & Company 0-4-0
Class A4b Steam Switching
Locomotive

A forerunner of the diesel-powered switchers working on today's railroads, this relatively little steam-driven machine has performed yeoman's service since its construction by Burnham, Williams & Company in 1903, most recently with Pennsylvania's Strasburg Railroad Company. Typical of most steam switchers (which appeared in configurations ranging from 0-4-0 to 0-10-0), both of its axles are driven, and it employs neither pilot nor trailing wheels. In 1904, No. 1187 could be seen toiling for the Philadelphia & Reading Railroad with the number it still wears today.

Chartered in 1833 as an affiliate of the Philadelphia & Reading Coal and Iron Company, the Philadelphia & Reading Railroad originated as an early coal-hauling line in southeastern Pennsylvania. In 1896 it became part of the Reading Company (not the Reading *Railroad*), which, by the mid-twentieth century (and after countless corporate permutations), operated a network of lines that also included the Central Railroad of New Jersey and the Lehigh Valley Railroad. During No. 1187's long career, the Philadelphia & Reading's main lines ran from Philadelphia to Williamsport and Harrisburg to Allentown, both via Reading.

1906
Greenbrier, Cheat & Elk Railroad No. 1

Lima Locomotive Works Three-Truck Shay-Type Steam Locomotive

Named for its inventor—Ohio-born mechanical engineer and logging man Ephraim Shay—the Shay-type steam engine ranks among the most unique locomotives ever built. Originally designed to haul loads over the treacherous tracks of logging operations, the odd-looking Shay employed a side-mounted, two- or three-cylinder, in-line vertical steam engine fed by a short, squat boiler. This powerplant, which drove several wheeled trucks by means of shafts, universal joints, and bevel gears, enabled logging trains to negotiate the steep grades and sharp curves characteristic of forest track.

Ohio's Lima Machine Works built the first engine of this type to Ephraim Shay's own specifications in 1880—thus marking the beginning not only of the Shay locomotive, but of the Lima Locomotive Works, later to become one of America's most important manufacturers of steam engines.

This three-truck, three-cylinder Shay is a Class 70-3 that ran for the Greenbrier, Cheat & Elk Railroad as Locomotive No. 1 in 1906, having been built the previous year. It is now part of the permanent collection of the Baltimore & Ohio Railroad Museum.

1907
Delaware & Hudson Railway Gondola No. 8148

American Car and Foundry Wooden Freight Gondola Car

About as basic as railroad "rolling stock" can get—with the possible exception of the flatcar—the open freight gondola has been used since the 1870s to haul practically anything that doesn't need protection from the elements. Essentially a low-sided, solid-bottomed rectangular box without a lid, the gondola was first developed to replace the small coal-carrying "jimmies" of railroading's early days. It was eventually replaced in coal and ore service by more specialized "hoppers," but continues up to the present day to transport everything from scrap metal to paving stone with little change in basic design.

In 1907, Gondola No. 8148—built a year earlier by American Car and Foundry of Berwick, Pennsylvania—was hauling bulk cargo for the historic Delaware & Hudson Railway, which grew from an early coal line to an important rail link to Canada before merging with Norfolk & Western in 1968.

1908
GVB (Graz, Austria) No. 120

Grazer Waggon Fabrik (Austria)
Single-Truck Tram

Although more a descendant of the horse-drawn car than of its railroading "cousin," the trolleycar (or street-car) is still essentially a train—albeit a smaller, lighter one—carrying passengers across town at relatively docile speeds, rather than whisking them over long distances. As trolleys developed they became essentially miniature railroad cars that rumbled along the streets of teeming American cities.

In Europe, however, the streetcar (better known as a "tram") evolved a little differently—perhaps even more directly descended from the horse car, but following a fairly standard formula. The typical European tram was a small, four-wheeled affair with an open platform, usually operated in trains of two or three cars.

The year 1908 saw the initial design of the single-truck tram pictured here, built by Grazer Waggon Fabrik and put into service with the GVB system

in the Austrian city of Graz the following year. Originally featuring an open driver's platform, this beautifully maintained four-wheeled tram has undergone many modifications over the years, but it continues to run to this day. Currently sporting the GVB livery of the late 1950s, No. 120 operates out of Maryland's National Capital Trolley Museum.

1909
Baltimore & Ohio Railroad No. 10

General Electric Corporation 0-4-0 (B-Type Switcher) Electric Locomotive

By the time the very early electric switching locomotive featured here was built by General Electric and put into service by the venerable Baltimore & Ohio Railroad in 1909, the grand old line had been in operation for more than 80 years.

Chartered in 1827 to cut a swath westward through the wilderness from Baltimore to the Ohio River, the B&O was neither America's first nor its largest railroad. But it was highly important to the commerce of the growing nation, and it continued to operate, through good times and bad, for the next 160 years!

Still wearing its B&O name and num-

ber (No. 10), this little (9.75-ton) 0-4-0 B-type box-cab locomotive saw long years of service as a Class CE-1 street trackage switcher on the docks of Fell's Point. Now housed in the B&O's remarkable Maryland museum, old No. 10 helps immerse visitors in the experience of nuts-and-bolts railroading during the early years of this century.

1910
SNCF (French National Railways) "Little Yellow Train"

Electric Narrow-Gauge
Passenger Train

As the century's second decade dawned, railroads were completing the process of "civilizing" an American West that had been wilderness just decades before. Southwestern narrow-gauge lines crisscrossed the mountains to haul precious ore, connect once-isolated towns, and treat passengers to breathtaking views.

In Europe, too, narrow-gauge railroads were providing access to remote areas. Launched in 1910 to help open up the rugged mountains of southern France, SNCF's jaunty "Little Yellow Train" (*Le Train Jaune*) is still in operation nearly 90 years later—transporting tourists enjoying the Continent's splendor.

Seen here winding its way along a one-meter-wide, electrified track through the Pyrenees in 1999, *Le Train Jaune* carries travelers over an engineering marvel of long tunnels and towering viaducts, through magnificent gorges, past craggy peaks, and across vast meadows to tiny villages along the way. This remarkable line—the highest in Europe—was begun in 1903 and eventually extended 40 miles from Villefranch-de-Conflent to Latour-de-Carol.

1910-1919

From little tank engines to massive Mikados, steam locomotives transport the products and resources on which vast personal empires are built. But when the railroads answer America's call to arms in the Great War, the U.S. government steps in and takes a hand.

1910

1911
Berlin Mills
Railway No. 7

Vulcan Iron Works 2-4-2T
(Saddle-Tank) Steam Locomotive

Beginning in the mid-nineteenth century, railroads had played a significant role in opening up remote areas in both eastern and western states to commerce and industry. Berlin Falls, in New Hampshire's White Mountains, is a perfect example of a once-isolated community linked to the outside world by the "iron horse."

In the early 1850s, what would eventually become Canada's Grand Trunk Railway began running through Berlin. About the same time, the origins of the Berlin Mills Company—including a private railway spur on which to ship lumber and paper products—were also springing up in the area. By the turn of the century, the Berlin Mills complex included lumber mills, paper mills, and an electrochemical plant—all of which used a few small steam locomotives to haul materials in and out.

The Vulcan Iron Works of Wilkes-Barre, Pennsylvania, built and delivered the squat little workhorse shown here as Berlin Mills Railway No. 7, in 1911. A 2-4-2T saddle-tank engine with 44-inch-diameter driving wheels, No. 7 and its sister locomotives were kept busy for decades hauling a variety of wood products out of the forests of New Hampshire. It has since retired to Pennsylvania's Steamtown National Historic Site.

1912
Washington
Terminal Company
No. 500-501

Industrial Works Steam-Powered Wrecking Crane and Crane Idler Car

A sobering reminder of what could happen to a train if something went wrong, the heavy wrecking crane was an unwanted but necessary fixture in American railyards. Dubbed the "big hook," it lifted rolling stock from the tracks after derailments or other accidents. When disaster struck, the steam-powered crane was pulled by a locomotive to the wreck site, where its crew rigged the derailed locos or cars and hoisted them back on the tracks or off to the siding. A flatcar accompanying the wrecker was equipped with spare railcar wheels to rerail and clear damaged cars.

A typical steam wrecker of this decade, Crane No. 500 was built by Industrial Works of Bay City, Michigan, and owned by the Pennsy prior to its service at the Washington Terminal Company. Capable of lifting up to 120 tons, it is shown here with its companion idler car, No. 501, at Baltimore's B&O Museum.

1913 Maine Central Railroad No. 519

Alco 2-8-0 (Consolidation)
Steam Locomotive

As it rolled out of Alco's Schenectady Works in February 1913—one of eight new 2-8-0 freight Consolidations ordered by the Maine Central Railroad that year—Locomotive No. 519 embarked on a long freight-hauling career that stretched into the 1950s.

Founded in 1862, the Maine Central Railroad gradually absorbed a number of smaller Maine roads—including the Leeds & Farmington, Portland & Kennebec, Maine Shore Line, Knox & Lincoln, and Moosehead lines—until it controlled nearly 500 miles of track throughout the state, with major centers in Portland and Bangor.

No. 519 was purchased as part of a series of new, high-boilered, low-tendered Consolidations destined to haul freight across the rocky hills of Maine, and it became one of the last three steam engines in the line's service. Today, No. 519's power is second among the four 2-8-0 locomotives in the Steamtown Foundation collection. When compared with another, Illinois Central No. 790 (see 1903), No. 519 can be seen to have larger drive wheels, a lower tender, and a longer wheelbase.

1914
Canadian National
Railways No. 47

Montreal Locomotive Works 4-6-4T
(Baltic-Tank) Steam Locomotive

A rather unique form of steam engine
especially designed for hauling
commuter trains, the suburban tank
locomotive became a familiar sight in
and around major North American
cities during the first few decades of
the new century. The term "tank"
referred to a locomotive with a coal
bin and water tank incorporated into
the engine design, eliminating the need
for a separate tender.

Early suburban tank engines running
in the metropolitan areas of Boston,
New York, and Chicago employed
2-4-4T, 2-6-4T, and 2-6-6T wheel
arrangements. The 4-6-4T Baltic type,
however, which incorporated a tank
into the 4-6-4 Hudson arrangement,
was first developed by Canada's
Montreal Locomotive Works for
Montreal suburban service with the
Grand Trunk Railway and later with
Canadian National Railways.

Montreal's Baltic design proved quite
successful and inspired the Central
Railroad of New Jersey to order six
4-6-4T locomotives from the Baldwin
Works for its own New York–area
suburban service in 1923. Of all the
suburban Baltics, however, only the
one seen here—Canadian National
Railways No. 47, photographed on
display at Steamtown National
Historic Site—has survived in the
United States.

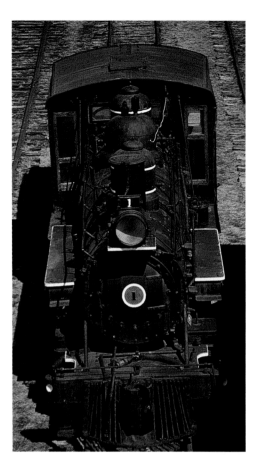

1915
Brooks-Scanlon
Corporation No. 1

Baldwin 2-6-2 (Prairie)
Steam Locomotive

Essentially an upgrade of the 2-6-0 Mogul—incorporating trailing wheels supporting a much larger firebox—the 2-6-2 Prairie-type steam locomotive was initially well-suited for the flat plains of the Midwest, hence its name.

Introduced around 1900, the Prairie type enjoyed great popularity on America's rails for a relatively short time. Soon outclassed and replaced on the main lines by larger, more powerful engines (especially the 2-8-2 Mikado and 4-6-2 Pacific), the 2-6-2 eventually found another niche—on the short lines of lumber companies working the flat forests of Florida and the West.

Outshopped by the Baldwin Works in 1914, the Prairie locomotive seen here completed its first year of service in 1915 as Locomotive No. 1 in the Carpenter-O'Brien Lumber Company's Florida mills. Within two years, however, the operation—and with it, Engine No. 1—was purchased by the Brooks-Scanlon Corporation, a Minnesota-based lumber firm.

Over the next four decades, No. 1 hauled and switched logging trains in Florida for Brooks-Scanlon and other companies, finally retiring in 1959. The old workhorse is seen here at Pennsylvania's Steamtown, still wearing its Brooks-Scanlon markings.

1916
Rahway Valley
Railroad No. 15

Baldwin 2-8-0 (Consolidation)
Steam Locomotive

This little Consolidation-type locomotive spent all its life in the service of two interesting little short-line railroads. Built in 1916, the engine first labored in the Tennessee hill country as No. 20 for the Oneida & Western Railroad.

Launched in 1913 to promote the development of lumber and coal interests in the region, the Oneida & Western was originally intended to run between Oneida, Tennessee, and Albany, Kentucky. After several years, however, the road fell short of expectations and settled into an existence as a 25-mile-long feeder line between East Jamestown, Tennessee, and Oneida, where it connected with the Cincinnati, New Orleans & Texas Pacific Railway. Little No. 20 chugged doggedly along those 25 miles of track for over two decades.

Strangely enough, New Jersey's Rahway Valley Railroad, incorporated in 1904, reportedly arose from its promoter's desire for easy access to his golf course in Summit! The road's other intended purpose—linking the Lehigh Valley and Jersey Central lines at one end with the Delaware, Lackawanna & Western at the other—never materialized, but the line persevered nonetheless. In 1937, Oneida & Western No. 20 became Rahway Valley No. 15, and served the New Jersey line faithfully and well before retiring in 1953.

1917
Canadian National
Railways No. 3254

Canadian Locomotive Company
2-8-2 (Mikado) Steam Locomotive

With smoke and steam billowing from
its stack on a clear Pennsylvania day,
Canadian National Railways
No. 3254—underway on the rails of
Steamtown National Historic Site—
is truly a sight to see. This mighty
octogenarian engine still regularly
hauls passengers there. But that's
just the most recent chapter in this
locomotive's fascinating history.

Manufactured in 1917 by the Kingston Works of the Canadian
Locomotive Company, this 2-8-2
Mikado first ran as No. 2854 for the
Canadian Government Railways, then
was renumbered as No. 3254 when
the Canadian Government Railways
was reorganized into Canadian
National Railways.

Maintenance records indicate that
No. 3254 was last outshopped in 1958,
so it is likely that this workhorse
served Canadian National Railways
for nearly 40 years, before retiring
from active service. The "Mike"
was bought and dismantled by a
Pennsylvania entrepreneur in
1961, but plans for its operation fell
through. It then spent some years
reassembled—but not bolted together—on the grounds of a motel!

In 1982, No. 3254 was finally put
back where it belonged—on the rails,
hauling excursion trains for the
Gettysburg Railroad. Five years later,
Steamtown acquired No. 3254—and
today, this remarkable engine delights
railfans on its Scranton tracks.

1918
Baltimore & Ohio
Railroad No. 4500

Baldwin 2-8-2 (Light Mikado)
Steam Locomotive

On the eve of America's entry into the Great War in 1917, the U.S. government doubted the ability of the nation's rail system to meet wartime demands. As a result, President Woodrow Wilson officially nationalized the railroads in December 1917, and in early 1918 the Railroad Control Act created an agency to take over their operation—the United States Railroad Administration.

Although the USRA's takeover was largely a disaster, the agency did produce a series of excellent steam locomotives that would set high standards for decades to come. Its roster included both light and heavy locomotives, switchers, and tenders, all designed by a team-up of Alco, Lima, and Baldwin. And the first USRA locomotive ever produced is seen here—a Baldwin-built, 2-8-2 Light Mikado assigned to the Baltimore & Ohio Railroad as No. 4500.

Eager to start off with a bang, the USRA strove to complete B&O No. 4500 in time for public display on Independence Day. After much hoopla—including the shipping of locomotive parts via Pullman car— the new "Mike" was unveiled to the American public on July 4, 1918.

No. 4500, its distinguished career now over, stands proudly at Baltimore's B&O Railroad Museum—a true piece of American railroading history.

1919
New Haven Trap
Rock Company
(Branford Steam
Railroad) No. 43

Vulcan Iron Works 0-4-0T
(Saddle-Tank) Steam Locomotive

Like another saddle-tank steam locomotive built by the Vulcan Iron Works of Wilkes-Barre, Pennsylvania (see 1911), the little 0-4-0T engine shown here labored mightily for an

industrial company with beginnings in the mid-nineteenth century.

The New Haven Trap Rock Company, incorporated in 1914 to quarry and haul paving rock from North Branford, Connecticut, was part of C. W. Blakeslee & Sons, a heavy construction business originally founded in 1844. But the short line that served the quarry had been established in the 1890s as the three-mile-long Damascus Railway, built to connect a Branford horse-trotting park with the New York, New Haven & Hartford Railroad. In 1903, it was linked to the quarry and renamed the Branford Steam Railroad. A decade later, both quarry and rail line became part of the New Haven Trap Rock Company.

Built in 1919, the 15-ton Locomotive No. 43 spent a career switching gondola cars loaded with trap rock around the quarry. The little engine hauled empty cars to be filled by railroad steam shovels, and pulled loaded cars to rock-crushing equipment. Officially retiring in 1959, No. 43 now spends its days at Pennsylvania's Steamtown.

1920
Canadian National
Railways No. 3377

Canadian Locomotive Company
2-8-2 (Mikado) Steam Locomotive

Canadian National Railways
No. 3377, like No. 3254—its sister
Mikado engine at Pennsylvania's
Steamtown, to which it is quite similar
(see 1917)—began life with another
number in the stable of the Canadian
Government Railways.

When originally built in 1919 by the
Canadian Locomotive Company's
Kingston Works, this 2-8-2 Mikado
carried the Canadian Government
Railroad No. 2977. But by 1920, after
the Canadian Government Railroad's
reorganization into the Canadian
National Railways, the nearly new
locomotive was relettered and served
as CNR No. 3377.

Although two years younger than
No. 3254, No. 3377 shares many
characteristics with the earlier
Mikado—both engines feature
identical cylinder and driver dimen-
sions, boiler pressure, and tractive
effort—but was designated as a
Class S-1-d locomotive due to minor
differences. Used mainly for hauling
freight during its four decades with
CNR, No. 3377 received a number
of upgrades over the years, including
a superheater, a mechanical stoker, a
feedwater heater, and large-capacity
air pumps for the brakes.

1920-1929

In the last decade of railroading's "Golden Age," steam-powered passenger trains are still the way to travel cross-country. Mighty "Mountains" and "Pacifics" haul opulent parlor cars and Pullman sleepers, while the first diesel-electrics appear quietly on the scene.

1921
Lowville & Beaver River Railroad No. 1923

Alco 2-8-0 (Consolidation) Steam Locomotive

The 2-8-0 Consolidation locomotive ranked among the most common on American railways early in the twentieth century. Nearly 150 have survived, including this one—shown here with its "snout" and stack gleaming white—whose colorful history began even *before* it took to the rails.

Alco originally built this spiffy little 2-8-0 in late 1920 as No. 8 for Compania Azucarera Central Reforma, a Cuban sugar plantation; a builder's photo showing its CACR markings still exists. But for some (perhaps political) reason remaining unclear to this day, the Cuban firm bailed out on the deal in early 1921.

After two years of unemployment, the engine became No. 1923 of the Lowville & Beaver River Railroad— a short line in New York's Adirondack region with a habit of numbering its locomotives by the year of purchase. It hauled passengers and freight on the L&BR till the 1950s, surviving an engine-house fire that nearly destroyed it in 1938.

1922
Public Service Electric & Gas Company No. 6816

H.K. Porter Company 0-6-0F (Fireless Switcher) Steam Locomotive

Although it resembles several fat saddle-tank steam locomotives featured elsewhere in this book, this squat little vehicle is actually one of only a few surviving examples of a unique development in steam locomotion—the fireless steam engine.

Operating on a principle first employed in New Orleans in the 1870s, the fireless engine carried no fuel or boiler to create steam. Rather, its cylinders derived pressure from live, high-temperature steam injected into the engine by a stationary boiler between runs. It was, in fact, a "rechargeable" locomotive, used mainly as an industrial switcher.

Manufactured in late 1922 by Pittsburgh's H. K. Porter Company, No. 6816 was delivered the next year to New Jersey's Public Service Electric Company (later PSE&G). It most likely spent decades switching coal cars at the utility's Essex generating plant in Newark, and is shown here enjoying its retirement at Pennsylvania's Steamtown National Historic Site.

1923

1923
Norwood & St. Lawrence Railroad No. 210

Alco 2-6-0 (Mogul) Steam Locomotive

The 2-6-0 wheel configuration, consisting of three driven axles led by a single pair of pilot wheels, first appeared in a steam locomotive built by the Rogers Works in Paterson, New Jersey, in 1863. During the next half-century, around 11,000 of the type—nicknamed "Mogul" for its power, which was considerable at the time—were eventually put into service. In 1923, exactly 60 years after that first Mogul appeared, this modern version was manufactured at Alco's Cooke Works in the same city.

Featuring an enclosed all-weather cab (clearly visible in these photographs), this hand-fired coal burner was built for the Norwood & St. Lawrence Railroad, an upstate New York short line operating since 1901, and by 1923 controlled by the St. Regis Paper Company. One of about 50 Moguls surviving today, No. 210 hauled passengers and freight (including milk, paper, and pulp) for the Norwood & St. Lawrence until 1956.

1924

1924
Strasburg
Railroad No. 90

Baldwin 2-10-0 (Decapod)
Steam Locomotive

Rumbling along with flags flapping and smoke and steam billowing from its stacks, Strasburg Railroad's massive Engine No. 90 is as exciting a sight now as when it hauled its first passenger train for the Great Western Railroad some 75 years ago.

Today, this venerable Decapod (a 2-10-0 arrangement featuring five driven axles) proudly hauls happy tourists on delightful 45-minute treks—including lunch and dinner service on restored vintage parlor and dining cars—through verdant Pennsylvania farmland for the Strasburg Railroad. Originally built by the Baldwin Works for the Great Western in 1924, No. 90 is one of several meticulously maintained steam locomotives still running daily for the busy Strasburg line, which ranks among the oldest and most popular steam tourist lines in the United States.

1924

Baldwin 4-8-2 (Mountain)
Steam Locomotive

By the century's quarter-mark, steam-locomotive technology was itself near-ly 100 years old and had entered what would become its final phase. The ongoing quest for locomotive power continued unabated in the 1920s. But since power depends on the size of the fire (and thus the firebox), it was sometimes sacrificed in favor of higher *tractive effort*—as in the case of the 4-8-2 Mountain arrangement.

Developed during the era of the U.S. Railroad Administration and illustrat-

ed by this gleaming engine built by Baldwin in 1925, the type's single trailing axle limited the size of its firebox. Its eight driving wheels, however, gave it the "oomph" to maintain considerable speed through mountainous terrain, and it proved quite successful throughout the United States and Canada.

One of five identical Mountains (all featuring cylindrical Vanderbilt ten-ders) bought by the Grand Trunk Western for passenger and freight ser-vice, No. 6039 raced across the line's Michigan and Indiana trackage until well into the 1950s.

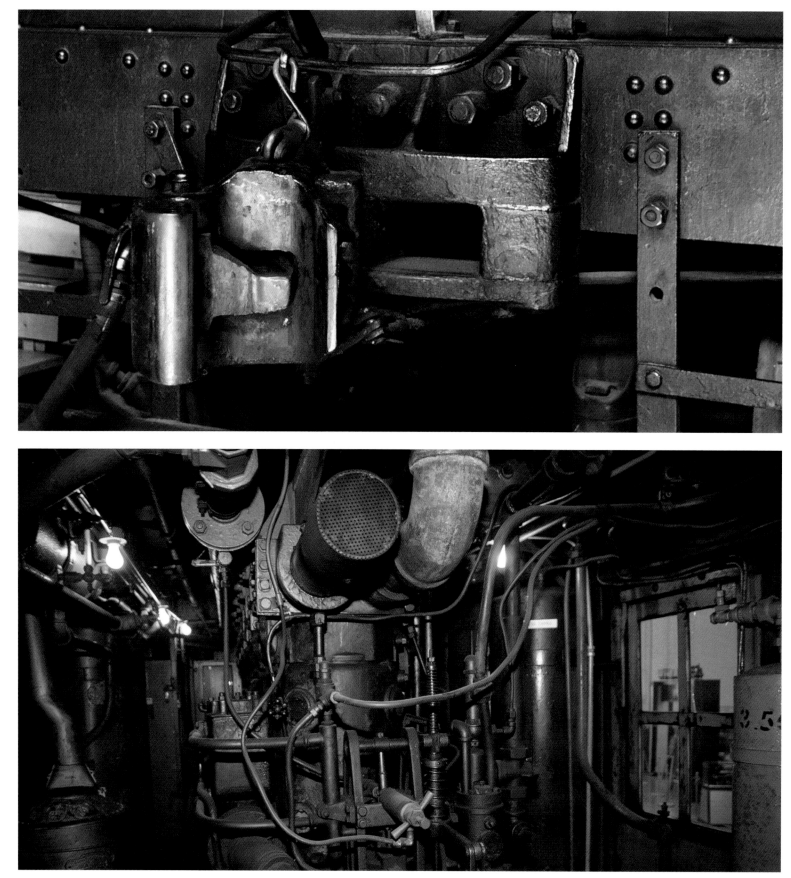

1926
Central Railroad
of New Jersey
No. 1000

Alco/GE/Ingersoll-Rand 300-hp
(Bo-Bo) Diesel-Electric Switching
Locomotive

Throughout railroading's first century,
steam power ruled the rails. But
science and industry never stopped
striving for more efficient methods
of motive power, experimenting with
both electric locomotion and internal
combustion. Eventually, principles
developed by Germany's Rudolph
Diesel evolved into the "diesel"
internal-combustion engine, in which
highly compressed fuel was injected
into the cylinder.

Employing a diesel engine to produce
tractive power, however, required a
complex transmission system. In the
early 1920s, three industrial giants
teamed up to create a solution: an
electric locomotive (manufactured by
Alco), powered by current from a
General Electric–built generator and
driven by an Ingersoll-Rand engine.

The historic result was the world's
first commercially successful diesel-
electric locomotive, a 300-hp Bo-Bo
switcher (with "Bo-Bo" indicating two
trucks, each with
two separately
driven axles).
Of the 24 units
produced between
1924 and 1928,
only two have
survived—includ-
ing Jersey Central
No. 1000, shown
here on display
at Baltimore's
B&O Railroad
Museum.

1927
E. J. Lavino &
Company No. 3

Alco 0-6-0T (Saddle-Tank) Steam
Switching Locomotive

Details of this saddle-tank industrial
steam switcher's operational history
are sketchy. Although both firms that
owned it are still in business, they are
vastly different from the companies
that operated this locomotive decades
ago.

The company that originally bottled
Maine's Poland Spring Water ordered
the engine new (as Poland Spring
Railroad Engine No. 2) in 1927 from
Alco's Schenectady, New York, plant.
Whether the firm actually used the
switcher on its bottling works' short
line or on the grounds of its Poland
Spring resort is unknown. Similarly,

records do not indicate when the
engine was sold to its second owner,
Pennsylvania blast-furnace operator
E. J. Lavino & Company, or how it
was used.

What's for certain is that the switcher—featuring a 1500-gallon saddle
tank, a one-ton coal bunker, and a
Lavino "L" logo (similar to that on
Lionel model trains)—was run by the
Lavino firm between 1950 and 1966,
when it was acquired by Steamtown
in Scranton, Pennsylvania.

1928
Baltimore & Ohio
Railroad No. 5300
President
Washington

Baldwin 4-6-2 (Pacific)
Steam Locomotive

Those old enough to have been passengers on the old Baltimore & Ohio
Railroad between its 100th anniversary in 1927 and its merger with the
Chesapeake & Ohio 30 years later
may well remember the experience
of riding behind the historic Pacific-
type engine seen here. Back in 1928,
B&O No. 5300—the *President
Washington*—was hailed as the most
modern locomotive on the American
rails.

The first of twenty similar locomotives commissioned for the B&O's
centennial and named for American
presidents, the *President Washington*
was completed by the Baldwin Works
in 1927. It made its public debut as the
centerpiece of a mile-long "pageant"
of transportation technology at the
"Fair of the Iron Horse" in Baltimore
that fall. In 1928, No. 5300 began its
first full year of service, launching a
distinguished 30-year career. No less
regal today, the venerable engine now
occupies a special place at Baltimore's
B&O Museum.

1929 Baldwin Locomotive Works No. 26

Baldwin 0-6-0 Steam
Switching Locomotive

Its 0-6-0 wheel arrangement—and
the brakeman's footboards across
its front and at the rear of its
slope-backed tender—identify this
locomotive as a typical switch engine
of the late 1920s. What made it
unique, however, was that instead
of being purchased and operated by
an industrial company, it was retained
by its manufacturer, the Baldwin
Locomotive Works, upon its construction in 1929.

That year, Baldwin expanded its
Eddystone plant to consolidate its
locomotive production there, and
No. 26 probably took part in that
effort. Ironically, 1929 also saw the
stock market crash that fostered the
Great Depression—and two decades
of struggle for the Baldwin Works.
When the company sold much of its
stock to Westinghouse in 1948, it also
sold this locomotive—to Ohio's
Jackson Iron and Steel Company,
which ran it into the 1970s. But as
the steam in the photo attests, old
No. 26 is still running today, at
Steamtown National Historic Site in
Scranton, Pennsylvania.

1930
Canadian Pacific Railway No. 2816

Montreal Locomotive Works 4-6-4
(Hudson) Class H-1-b
Steam Locomotive

Streamlined power appeared to be the
order of the day for the world's railroads as the 1930s dawned, and the
Canadian Pacific Railway proved no
exception. In a bid to "push the enve-
lope" past the performance of CP's
then top-of-the-line Class G-3 Pacifics
(4-6-2), CP's motive-power
chief Henry B. Bowen
launched the development
of a new class of powerful
steam locomotives shortly
after his appointment in the
fall of 1928.

The new, streamlined
engines would utilize a 4-6-4
wheel arrangement (with
two pilot and two trailing
axles) to accommodate a
superheater, an enlarged

firebox, and a mechanical stoker, all
designed to increase power. Dubbed
the "Hudson" type (Class H-1) and
numbered from 2800 to 2805, the first
of this beautiful new breed rolled off
the Montreal Works assembly line in
late 1929. More arrived the following
year, including CP No. 2816—shown
here as it looks today—completed in
December 1930.

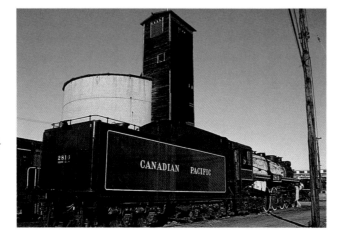

1930

1930-1939

Although the Depression ruins many railroads, others continue to thrive. Powerful new steam, diesel, and electric locomotives all get the Art Deco–inspired streamline treatment, and innovations like the Bullet car, the GG-1, and the E-series Streamliners make their debut.

1931
Pennsylvania Railroad No. 6755

Altoona Works (PRR) 4-8-2
(Mountain) Class M-1
Steam Locomotive

Throughout the "Golden Age of Railroading" (roughly 1880–1930), the Pennsylvania Railroad earned a reputation as the "Standard Railroad of the World." Expanding rapidly after its birth in 1854, by 1900 "the Mighty Pennsy" controlled much of the East's long-distance rail traffic— and it would continue to dominate passenger service and haul a large share of the country's industrial product right through the 1920s.

To complement the famous K-4 class of 4-6-2 Pacifics that had spearheaded its express passenger service since the 'teens, the Pennsy launched its M-1

class of 4-8-2 Mountain-type locomotives in the twenties. The massive M-1b shown here, PRR No. 6755, was built at the line's own Altoona Works in 1930, and by 1931 it had begun a career of dual service that would stretch into the 1950s. Still proudly displaying its "keystone" at the Railroad Museum of Pennsylvania, it is the largest Pennsy steam locomotive preserved today.

1932
Philadelphia & Western No. 205
Bullet Car

J. G. Brill Company Double-Truck
Interurban Trolleycar

Looking for all the world like a true "child of the thirties," J. G. Brill's revolutionary Bullet interurban trolleycar shows the great influence that aerodynamic testing had on high-speed transportation designs of the decade's early Art Deco years. In fact, echoes of the striking, stream-lined design of the aluminum-bodied Bullet—which was very likely the first trolley ever tested in a wind tunnel—would be found, a bit later in the decade, in such railroad locomotives as the steam-driven Burlington Zephyr and the electric-powered GG-1.

When the Philadelphia & Western unveiled the Bullet on its mainline interurban service in late 1931 and early 1932, in the depths of the Depression, ridership actually increased due to the car's impressive 85-mph speed. Although this particular Bullet car, still awaiting restoration, may perhaps seem a shadow of its former self, other examples of this remarkable design were still running for SEPTA, Philadelphia & Western's successor, 60 years after their introduction!

1933
Boston & Maine
Railroad No. 3713

Lima Locomotive Works 4-6-2
(Pacific) Steam Locomotive

A particularly fine example of stream-lined steam, Boston & Maine Railroad's Engine No. 3713 was one of five brand-new Pacific-type locomotives ordered by the B&M in 1933. Classified P-4-a and numbered 3710 through 3714, the Pacifics were completed and delivered to the rail-road in 1934 by Ohio's Lima Works, which had lately earned a reputation for building impressively powerful, "modern" steam locomotives.

Designed to run at a normal speed of 70 mph, No. 3713 soon became a mainstay of B&M's mainline passenger service. In 1937 the engine picked up a title—*The Constitution*—as a result of a promotional contest invit-ing New England schoolchildren to name the B&M's locomotives. So named, No. 3713 continued to propel travelers—and, during World War II, many a soldier aboard a troop train—across the railroad's trackage in Massachusetts, New York, Maine, and Vermont until retiring in 1958.

1934 Pennsylvania Railroad No. 4800

Baldwin/General Electric (2-Co-Co-2)
Class GG-1 Electric Locomotive

With the world gripped by a desperate Depression, few corporations besides the Pennsylvania Railroad could have even considered as costly a proposition as electrifying one of its main lines. But this was "the Mighty Pennsy"—and by 1934, electrification between New York and Washington was almost complete! Now what the "Standard Railroad of the World" needed was the electric express passenger locomotive—and that was the GG-1.

Developed from a sound 2-Co-Co-2 configuration (two sets of three driven axles, with a pair of pilots on either end) with a stylish body by famed industrial designer Raymond Loewy, the GG-1 was a streamlined dream. Capable of continuously producing close to 5000 hp and a top speed of 100 mph, the remarkable locomotive was yet another jewel in Pennsy's already heavily laden crown. Nearly 150 were produced between 1935 and 1943, either by the PRR's Altoona shops, Baldwin, or General Electric. And you're looking at the historic prototype—PRR No. 4800, completed in August 1934.

DANGER: DO NOT TOUCH

1934

1935
Pennsylvania
Railroad No. 5690

**Altoona Works (PRR) Class B1
Electric Switching Locomotive**

As several previous entries in this
book illustrate (see 1909, 1926, and
1934), electric motive power had been
employed by America's railways in a
wide variety of situations since the late
nineteenth century. The nation's first
public railroad, the Baltimore & Ohio,
also became the first to electrify part

1936
Bullard Company
No. 2

**H. K. Porter Company 0-4-0T
(Saddle-Tank) Steam Locomotive**

Aside from the fact that it arrived at
the Bridgeport, Connecticut, plant of
the Bullard Machine Tool Company

in October 1937 and was used there
for nearly two decades, little is known
of the actual operational history of this
tiny saddle-tank locomotive. But histo-
rian Gordon Chappell—National Park
Service chronicler of the locomotive
collection at Steamtown N.H.S.,
where Bullard No. 2 now resides—
has pieced together a fascinating story
of how the little engine came to be.

Chappell reports that the Steamtown
files contained a 1913 H. K. Porter
Company catalog with inked notations
mentioning "Bullard," and alterations
to the specifications of an 0-4-0 industrial locomotive that match the actual
specs of the much smaller Bullard
engine. Apparently, in 1936 or 1937,
someone at the Bullard Company had
used a 23-year-old catalog to "design"
and order this locomotive, which,
according to yet another notation, was
received on October 25, 1937!

of a main line operation in 1895. And
after having used electric switchers
and other equipment for specific
purposes since the turn of the century,
the Pennsylvania Railroad adopted
its first electric express passenger
engine—the famous GG-1—in
anticipation of its first electrified
main line between New York and
Washington in 1934.

It was for use on just such an
electrified line that the PRR's Altoona
shops produced this Class B1 electric
switcher in December 1934. Put into
service in 1935, No. 5690 labored
faithfully on the Pennsy for many
years before retiring to Strasburg's
Railroad Museum of Pennsylvania.

H I O

1937
Baltimore & Ohio
Railroad No. 51

General Motors EMD (A1A-A1A)
Class EA Diesel-Electric Locomotive

Since the first practical application of
diesel-electric motive power in the
mid-1920s, the winds of change had
been softly blowing for American railroading. But they kicked into gale
force when General Motors—after
becoming involved in locomotive production in the early thirties—opened
its new Electro-Motive Division plant
at La Grange, Illinois, in 1936, for
the stated purpose of building a new
generation of express passenger diesel-
electric locomotives.

EMD's first new engines—1800-hp
units with an A1A-A1A wheel
arrangement—rolled off the La
Grange assembly line in 1937. Dubbed
the "E" (or "Streamliner") series and
offered with ("A") or without ("B")
a driver's cab, they were the first fully
streamlined diesel locomotives on the
American rails. The Baltimore &
Ohio bought the first six, designating
them Class EA and EB. One of those
historic EA units, No. 51, served until
1953 and is seen here in retirement
at Baltimore's B&O Museum.

1938
Canadian Pacific
Railway No. 2929

Canadian Locomotive Company
4-4-4 ("Jubilee") Class F-1-a
Steam Locomotive

Seen here wearing a partial blanket
of snow is a uniquely Canadian
locomotive, of a type that never
caught on in the United States—
the 4-4-4. Trials of 4-4-4's by the
Philadelphia & Reading in 1915 and
the Baltimore & Ohio in 1934 met
with little success. So it was left to the
Canadian Pacific Railway to develop
an impressive new series of streamlined 4-4-4's, introduced along with
the railway's High-Speed Local
Service in 1936.

Nicknamed "Jubilee" and designated
Class F-2-a, the Canadian Pacific's
new engines (Nos. 3000 to 3005)
featured feedwater heaters and
mechanical stokers, and spearheaded
high-speed runs between Calgary and
Edmonton, Toronto and Detroit, and
Montreal and Quebec. In 1938, however, Canadian Pacific backtracked
somewhat to produce a second series
of slightly smaller Jubilees (Nos. 2901
to 2929), designated F-1-a. Of these,
only the last two survive today: No.
2928 at Quebec's National Railway
Museum, and this one—No. 2929—
photographed at Steamtown, in
Scranton, Pennsylvania.

1939
Pennsylvania
Power & Light
Company No. 4094

Heisler Locomotive Works 0-8-0F
(Fireless Switcher) Steam
Locomotive

As mentioned earlier in this book (see
1922), the fireless locomotive, which
drew live steam from a stationary
boiler and was therefore "rechargeable," was hardly a common sight on
the American rails and was most
often used in industrial settings. This
particular example, however, is even
more unique than most, for a variety
of reasons.

Produced by the Heisler Locomotive
Works in 1939 for switching service
at facilities of the Pennsylvania
Power & Light Company, No. 4094
employed an 0-8-0 wheel configuration, the only fireless engine ever to do
so. It was also the largest locomotive
of its kind ever built, and was, in fact,
on exhibit for a time at the 1939–1940
New York World's Fair. Today,
PP&L No. 2 can be found in yet
another exhibit—on the grounds of
the Railroad Museum of Pennsylvania
at Strasburg.

The War Years— The 1940s

A dramatic evening scene depicts a common sight in what may have been American railroading's finest hour: mobilizing a nation for war. At Pennsylvania's Steamtown National Historic Site, World War II re-enactors and railroad workers recreate the activity of loading troops and freight for a nighttime departure—a scene repeated countless thousands of times between 1941 and 1945.

With a legendary "Big Boy" locomotive looming in the background, World War II re-enactors flash the "V for Victory" in a recreation of a photograph that appeared in LIFE magazine during the war years.

1940
Union Pacific
Railroad No. 4012

Alco 4-8-8-4 (Big Boy)
Steam Locomotive

Created in 1863 to build the Transcontinental Railroad westward from
the Missouri, the mighty Union
Pacific Railroad endured decades
of boom, bust, and bankruptcy to
re-emerge in the twentieth century as
a modern, innovative railroad linking
the cities of the American West.
Although Union Pacific had already
introduced several revolutionary
streamlined diesel-electrics into
regular service during the 1930s, it
still had one great steam locomotive
left up its sleeve: the legendary 4-8-8-4
Big Boy.

Named by an unknown mechanic
who wrote "Big Boy" on one of the
new engines, the first of only twenty-
five 4-8-8-4's ever built rolled out of
the Alco plant in 1940, among the
largest and heaviest steam locomotives
in history. They were made to haul
Union Pacific's heavy freights across
mountain and desert between
Cheyenne, Wyoming, and Ogden,
Utah, a feat which the Big Boy
shown here—No. 4012, built in
1941—performed for more than 20
years, logging over a million miles
before retiring in 1962.

1940

1940-1949

The world is plunged into yet another global conflict, and the nation's railroads mobilize at home and overseas to make an Allied victory possible. But at war's end, the success of the diesel locomotive signals the eventual end of "big steam" on America's rails.

1941
Chesapeake & Ohio Railway No. 1604

Lima Locomotive Works 2-6-6-6 (Allegheny) Steam Locomotive

As World War II entered its second full year in Europe, America sat on the sidelines, gearing up for its inevitable entry into the conflict. And the nation's railroads played a vital role in that mobilization, hauling countless personnel and ever-increasing volumes of raw materials and industrial products needed for defense.

By the 1940s, the venerable Chesapeake & Ohio Railway had become a major American railroad and one of the world's leading shippers of bituminous coal. As befitting its stature, the Chessie commissioned the Lima Works to build an enormous new locomotive capable of hauling heavy coal cars ("drags") over rugged Eastern mountains.

In 1941, Lima delivered the result. The humongous Allegheny employed a unique 2-6-6-6 wheel arrangement and weighed in at nearly 390 tons, making it perhaps the heaviest, most powerful steam locomotive ever built. Chesapeake & Ohio No. 1604, shown here at the B&O Museum, is one of only two surviving examples of this remarkable engine.

1942
U.S. Army Corps of Engineers No. 8077

Alco Class RS-1 (1000-hp)
Diesel-Electric Switching Locomotive

WAR!! After the Japanese attack on Pearl Harbor in December 1941, there was hardly an idle moment for anyone working on America's railroads—be they civilian or soldier, over here or "over there." Everyone and everything was on the move, "on the double"—millions of U.S. Armed Forces personnel; the equipment they would fight with; the food they would eat; the countless tons of raw materials, produce, and industrial product that supplied the Allied war machine. It was a monumental job, but the railroads were up to it.

Early in 1942, the U.S. military and the rail industry embarked on an extraordinary cooperative effort to pull off a victory over the enemy. Virtually every manufacturer took part. Alco is represented here by a 126-ton, Class RS-1 diesel-electric road switcher built for the U.S. Army Corps of Engineers in December 1942. With its hooded body and handrails for easy access, this 1000-hp engine was a harbinger of things to come.

1943
Pullman Company No. 7437

Pullman-Standard Car Manufacturing Company Troop Sleeper

From the moment America entered World War II, the movement of troops ranked among the rail system's chief priorities. Under Office of Defense Transportation edicts, nonessential civilian passenger traffic was restricted, and existing sleeping cars were reassigned to military tasks. And when the Army ordered construction of new troop sleepers to its own specifications, it naturally turned to the firm whose name had become synonymous with the railroad sleeping car—Pullman.

A decade after first tinkering with railroad sleeping cars in 1850s Chicago, cabinetmaker George Mortimer Pullman founded a company that would eventually become the world's largest builder of railroad cars. Seventy-five years later, that same company began producing thousands of Pentagon-designed, "no-frills" troop sleepers with 30 sets of triple-decker bunks straddling a center aisle to accommodate 90 soldiers. A typical Pullman troop car—No. 7437, built between 1943 and 1945—is shown here. Like many cars of its type, it was most likely used for track-maintenance work after the war.

1944
New York, Chicago & St. Louis Railroad (Nickel Plate Road) No. 757

Lima Locomotive Works 2-8-4
(Berkshire) Class S-2
Steam Locomotive

The 2-8-4 Berkshire-type locomotive originated in the mid-1920s, when Lima Locomotive Works designer Will Woodard looked to improve on the performance of the popular 2-8-2 Mikado type. Woodard's solution, a more powerful 2-8-4, was successfully tested in Massachusetts' Berkshire Hills—hence the name—and first went into service with the New York Central.

Seen here at the Railroad Museum of Pennsylvania at Strasburg, No. 757 was one of eight identical Class S-2 Berkshires outshopped by Lima to the "Road" in August 1944; another locomotive from that group, No. 759, resides nearby at Steamtown.

1945
Pennsylvania Railroad No. 5901

General Motors EMD (A1A-A1A)
Class EP20 (E7) Diesel-Electric
Locomotive

Resplendent in its maroon-and-yellow Pennsy livery, PRR No. 5901—an E7 diesel-electric built by General Motors Electro-Motive Division in 1945—personifies the "diesel revolution" that overtook America's railroads in the years following World War II. Certainly, steam locomotives and diesel-electrics had been operating in peaceful coexistence since the 1930s—especially during the war years, when any engine that would run was frantically pressed into service. But after V-J Day, the country's tired, rundown locomotive fleets needed new blood—and GM's diesels supplied it.

Among the finest Berkshire locomotives ever built were those of the Nickel Plate Road (officially the New York, Chicago & St. Louis), including several series produced by Lima between 1942 and 1944. These beautiful machines performed yeoman's service for the line in the thick of the war years, hauling "men and materiel" for America's "arsenal of democracy," and enjoyed long careers thereafter.

After restrictions halting passenger engine production were lifted in 1945, GM's EMD jumped into the business of building a new generation of diesel passenger locomotives for a prosperous post-war America. The first of these were the E7's, which featured many improvements over the E series of the thirties. The handsome E7 seen here was one of 60 delivered to the Pennsy shortly after the war.

1946
Chesapeake & Ohio
Railway No. 490

Huntington Shops (C&O) 4-6-4
(Streamlined Hudson) Class L-1
Steam Locomotive

The sleek lines of Chesapeake & Ohio
Engine No. 490 reflect the penchant
for streamlining that permeated locomotive design in the 1930s and 1940s.
The handsome yellow engine looks
very much like the M-1 steam turbo-
electric streamliners C&O launched
for a post-war daytime service—but
it's not. It's actually a Class L-1,
Hudson-type 4-6-4 steam locomotive
that was, in fact, rebuilt and streamlined at C&O's Huntington, West
Virginia, shops in 1946 from a much
earlier Class F-19 4-6-2 Pacific.

The railroad created the L-1's to join
the three M-1 turbo-electrics on the
daytime streamliner *The Chessie*
and had Baldwin build five brand-new
4-6-4s, intending to streamline them
as well. Ironically, the expensive
turbos bombed and were scrapped
within several years, as was the
entire streamliner project. The new
Hudsons went on to successful
careers "as is." No. 490, shown here
at the B&O Museum, is all that's left
of the Chessie's great streamlining
experiment.

1947
Reading Company No. 2124

Baldwin/Reading Company Shops
4-8-4 (Northern) Class T-1
Steam Locomotive

A mighty locomotive with a fascinating history, Reading Company No. 2124 has enjoyed several interesting careers. It began life as a Class I-10a, 2-8-0 Consolidation, built for Reading by Baldwin in the mid-1920s. Twenty years later, the railroad decided to rebuild 20 older 2-8-0's into virtually new 4-8-4 Northerns, this engine among them.

Northern-type 4-8-4's first served with the Northern Pacific (hence the name) in 1926, and pleased the NP so

Thus revitalized, the "new" Class T-1 Northern became Reading No. 2124 and ran regular service until 1959— when it became famous both as a movie star (appearing in the film "From the Terrace") and as the first locomotive used to pull excursion trains for railfans in the celebrated "Reading Rambles."

much it never again used another type. To convert the older locomotives into modern Northerns in 1947, Reading kept the cylinders and the huge firebox; stretched the boiler; replaced the underframes, wheels, and other parts; and added a feedwater heater and booster.

1948
New York, New Haven & Hartford Railroad No. 0673

Alco Class RS-1 (1000-hp) Diesel-Electric Switching Locomotive

When Alco first introduced its RS-1 diesel-electric road switcher in 1941, American railroads were skeptical. Previous diesels performed a single service, but the RS-1 could handle it all—passenger, yard switching, or road freight duty. Although the first RS-1 entered service on the Rock Island Railroad in 1941, the road switcher's value wasn't apparent until its distinguished wartime service (see 1942) made railmen take notice.

The history of this engine—shown here as New York, New Haven & Hartford No. 0673 at Connecticut's Danbury Railway Museum—is especially interesting because no such RS-1 actually worked on the New Haven line. Built by Alco in 1948, this switcher served with the Illinois Terminal, the Gulf, Mobile & Ohio, the Illinois Central Gulf, and the Green Mountain. Now used by the Danbury Railway Museum for switching and excursion duties, it has been painted to resemble the New Haven's own RS-1's when delivered new in 1948.

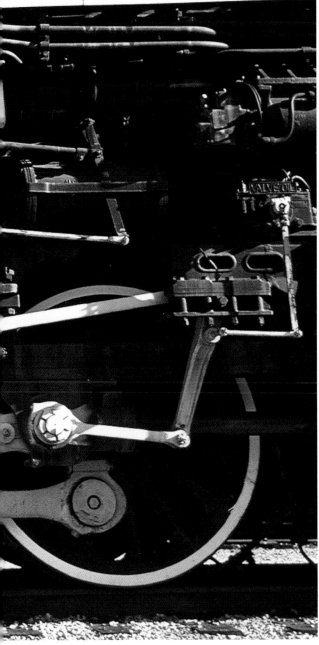

1949
Chesapeake & Ohio
Railway No. 1309

Baldwin 2-6-6-2 (Articulated
Compound Mallet-Type) Class H-6
Steam Locomotive

America at mid-century was prosperous, proud, and powerful—and the steam locomotive had helped make it so. But since its last show of strength in World War II, the steam engine had been on its way out, replaced by cleaner, more efficient, more economical diesel-electrics. The "Age of Steam" was essentially over.

In 1949, the Baldwin Locomotive Works built its last steam locomotive for domestic use in the United States: this mighty 2-6-6-2 compound Mallet type, Chesapeake & Ohio No. 1309. The first American version of Anatole Mallet's nineteenth-century articulated compound locomotive design— featuring two sets of driving wheels mounted on separate hinged frames—

had appeared on the Baltimore & Ohio in 1903. The Chessie began employing large Mallet types in the 1920s, and continued the practice into the 1940s. Seen here in all its glory at the B&O Museum, C&O No. 1309 represented the legendary Baldwin company's final efforts in steam locomotive production for an American railroad.

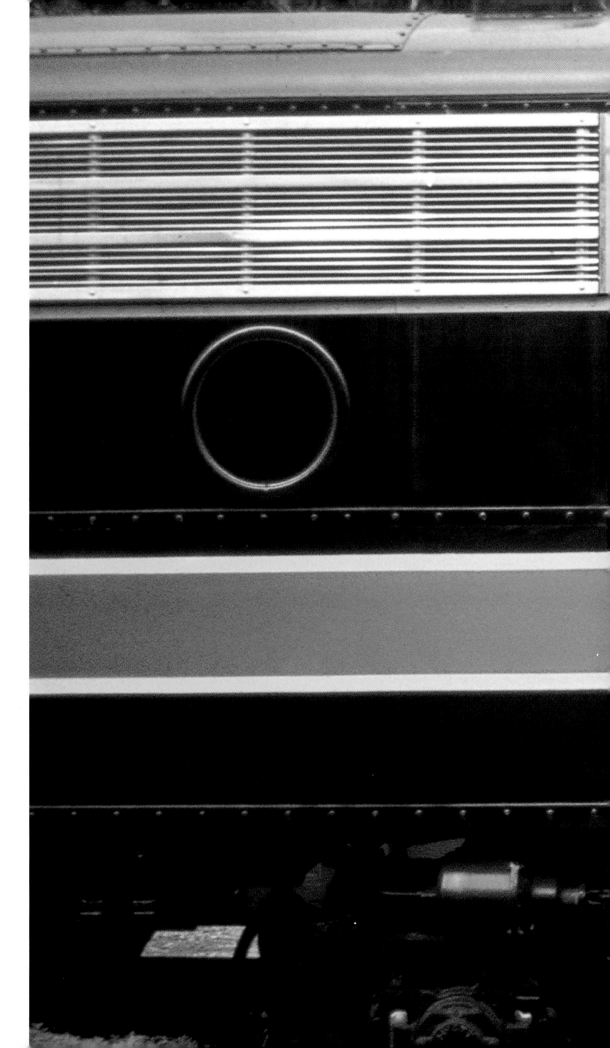

1950
Reading Company
No. 902

General Motors EMD (Bo-Bo) Class FP-7 Diesel-Electric Locomotive

Here you see a beautiful example of perhaps the most recognizable all-purpose diesel locomotive series ever built—Electro-Motive Division's 1500-hp F series, which debuted in 1939 and continued well into the 1950s. With its clean, sleek lines making the railroads' colorful postwar liveries practical, the F-7 model represented here was, in fact, the best-selling carbody diesel in history.

Originally designed to bring diesel power to the forefront of freight hauling on the eve of World War II, the streamlined F locomotives impressed the industry with their power and reliability, and were later used in passenger service as well. They stayed in production through the fifties.

In 1949, EMD introduced the first F-7s, which were produced through 1953 and performed nobly in dual service as late as the 1980s. The gleaming engine shown here—Reading Lines No. 902, built in 1950—is an FP-7 version, which featured a steam generator for heating passenger cars.

1950-1959

Wearing colorful postwar livery, diesel motive power by General Motors and Alco rules the rails in the prosperous fifties. But as more Americans take to the road—and to the sky—fewer and fewer are traveling by train. And the railroads begin feeling the pinch.

1951
Erie Railroad
No. 835

General Motors EMD (A1A-A1A)
Class E-8 Diesel-Electric Locomotive

As the "Age of Steam" vaporized into
history in the years following World
War II, General Motors Electro-
Motive Division roared "full steam
ahead" (an ironic term, perhaps) into
the 1950s as the leading producer of
diesel-electric motive power for
America's railroads. After setting
the standard for streamlined express
passenger diesel locomotives with
its highly successful 2000-hp E-7
engine (see 1945), EMD introduced
its follow-up in 1949: the handsome,
side-portholed 2250-hp E-8.

Along with GM's other E-series
locomotives—including its slightly
larger sister, the 2400-hp E-9, appearing in 1954—the E-8 was among the
fastest diesel locomotives in the world,
capable of reaching nearly 120 mph
(although rarely run over 100 mph).
GM sold 457 E-8 units to U.S. railroads. The one shown on the left in
the photo above, Erie No. 835, completed its first full year of service in
1951, having rolled off EMD's La
Grange assembly the previous year.

1952 Western Maryland Railway No. 236

General Motors EMD (Bo-Bo) Class F-7A Diesel-Electric Locomotive

Introduced by EMD in 1949, the F-7A freight locomotive turned out to be just what many U.S. railroads needed as they approached mid-century and the impending eclipse of steam power. All told, over 2300 of these reliable diesels were purchased throughout North America.

And for the Western Maryland Railway, which hauled a great deal of freight along with its Baltimore-Chicago passenger service, the F-7A—represented by WM No. 236, built in 1952 and shown here at the B&O Museum—was a perfect match.

Chartered in 1852, the Western Maryland extended westward from Baltimore to points in Pennsylvania and the coalfields of West Virginia. Dubbed the "Mason and Dixon Line" because it roughly parallels that famous North-South boundary, it was commandeered by Union forces during the Civil War and played a significant role in the conflict. More than a century later, the expanded WM was still hauling tonnage over steep Allegheny grades, a task for which the F-7A was well suited.

1953   Western Maryland Railway No. 195

Alco RS-3 (1600-hp) Diesel-Electric Switching Locomotive

Although Alco's original RS-1 diesel-electric road switcher stayed in production for an incredible 19 years after its introduction in 1941, the Schenectady, New York, manufacturer soon unveiled two powerful follow-ups to the groundbreaking 1000-hp locomotive. The 1500-hp RS-2 appeared in 1946; its 1600-hp cousin, the RS-3, superseded it in 1950 and remained in production through 1956, with 1265 units put into both freight and passenger service in the United States alone. Both locomotives became familiar sights on the rails, and some are still chugging along on short lines today.

Shown here at its present home at Baltimore's B&O Railroad Museum, this RS-3 was built in 1953 for the Western Maryland Railway. As No. 195, it rendered years of faithful service on the busy line's trackage through the Appalachians and Alleghenies, now part of the CSXT (formerly Chessie) rail system.

1954
Remington Arms
Company No. 2

Mack Company (170-hp) FCD-II
Diesel-Electric Self-Propelled Railbus

After 45 years, this unique railcar has
yet to perform the passenger service
for which it was designed. And its
fascinating, checkered history reflects
the corporate chaos that plagued
America's railroads in the 1950s.

Remington Arms No. 2 began life as
New Haven Railroad No. 15, one of
ten 170-hp, four-axle diesel-electric
railbuses built by the Mack Company
in 1954. Named "FCD" for New
Haven Railroad President Frederick
C. Dumaine, Sr., No. 15 and its
sisters were scheduled to debut that
year, but a takeover of the New
Haven killed the project.

In 1962, No. 15 and another FCD-II
were sold to the Remington Arms
Company and converted to haul
munitions at the firm's Bridgeport,
Connecticut, plant. Both were retired
and sold in 1985. One, rebuilt as a
subway test car, still lurks beneath the
streets of New York City; No. 2 was
donated to the Danbury Railway
Museum, which plans to restore it to
operational condition as New Haven
No. 15. It is the only FCD railbus
currently in a U.S. museum.

1955
Baltimore & Ohio
Railroad No. 633

General Motors EMD (Bo-Bo)
SW-900 Diesel-Electric
Switching Locomotive

While establishing itself as a leading
manufacturer of diesel motive power
with its landmark E- and F-series
locomotives, GM's Electro-Motive
Division also entered the switcher
market with the SW-1. Introduced in
1939, the 600-hp SW-1 was built
around GM's 567 diesel powerplant,
and it stayed in production until 1953.
It spawned a series of switchers
destined to cement EMD's reputation
for excellent diesel power, including
the 1000-hp NW-2, the 1200-hp SW-7
and SW-9, and the 800-hp SW-8.

In 1954, EMD began designating
locomotive models according to their
horsepower and introduced a line
of switchers in 600-hp, 900-hp, and
1200-hp versions. Among these was
the popular 900-hp SW-900, produced
through 1965. Built in 1955, the
SW-900 seen here began service as
B&O No. 633, but spent much of its
35-year career as No. 9408. It was
later restored to its original livery by
the B&O Museum, where it resides
today.

1956   Florida East Coast Railway (FEC) No. 663

General Motors EMD (Bo-Bo) GP-9 Diesel-Electric Locomotive

Seeking to increase its substantial diesel market share in the 1940s, General Motors EMD endeavored to bridge the gap between its successful streamlined E and F locomotives on the one hand, and its SW and NW switchers on the other. These efforts yielded the costly BL ("branch line") locomotive in 1948, but the next year developed the first true general-purpose diesel—the 1500-hp GP-7—followed in 1954 by the almost identical 1750-hp GP-9.

Although EMD's chief engineer Richard Dilworth sought a simple, economical locomotive that was so "ugly" it would be gladly sent any-where, the "Geep's" functional cab was actually not bad-looking, and contributed to the series' success. Its hood allowed easy access for main-tenance, and the offset cabin offered good visibility for crews, who immedi-ately took to the design. Both the GP-7 and GP-9 (produced from 1954 to 1959) became big sellers, and many—like FEC No. 633, a GP-9 built in 1956—were still on the road in the 1980s.

1957
New York, New
Haven & Hartford
Railroad
No. 140-141
Roger Williams

Experimental Matched Diesel-Electric Passenger Locomotive (Modified Budd RDC)

At one time among the Northeast's greatest railroads, the New York, New Haven & Hartford Railroad (or simply the New Haven), which was created in 1872 by merger of the New York & New Haven and Hartford & New Haven lines, served as the rail gateway to New England.

In the 1950s, the New Haven was essentially bled lifeless by takeovers and the policies of executive Patrick McGinnis. During this period the New Haven adopted the bold red, white, and black "McGinnis livery" seen here on New Haven No. 140-141, an experimental diesel-electric multiple-unit train called *Roger Williams*. Built in 1957, these matched units ran on New Haven's shoreline service as a six-car train of modified Budd rail diesel cars (RDCs). After the New Haven's demise in the 1960s, this combination became Penn Central No. 83-84, then Amtrak No. 27-28. It has since been restored to its original livery and is displayed as shown at the Danbury Railway Museum.

1958
New York, Chicago & St. Louis Railroad (Nickel Plate Road) No. 514

General Motors EMD (Bo-Bo) GP-9
Diesel-Electric Locomotive

Because its fabled Berkshire steam locomotives continued to outpace competitors' diesels well into the 1950s, the Nickel Plate Road (officially the New York, Chicago & St. Louis Railroad) was in no hurry to completely dieselize its operations. When it finally got around to doing that, the line purchased a score of new EMD GP-9's, numbered 510 to 529—one of which, No. 514, built in 1958, is shown here.

When the Nickel Plate Road was merged into the Norfolk & Western a few years later (in 1966), No. 514 was renumbered as Norfolk & Western No. 2514. The Norfolk & Western later became part of today's vast Norfolk Southern Corporation, which retired the GP-9 in 1985 and traded it to the Steamtown Foundation. Although the engine was restored to its original Nickel Plate Road livery and number, it was later repainted as a fictional Lackawanna locomotive for excursion duty at Pennsylvania's Steamtown National Historic Site.

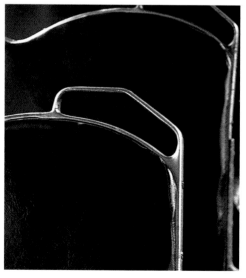

1959
Oakland Bay Rapid
Transit No. 167

Electric Articulated Suburban
Commuter Train

In contrast to the many "firsts"
chronicled in these pages, we here
pay tribute to a "last": the final year
of operation for a proud veteran of
over 20 years' service on the suburban
rails of Northern California. Since its
debut in the 1930s, this articulated
electric commuter train tirelessly
hauled countless passengers in the
Bay Area. But in 1959, Oakland Bay
Rapid Transit decommissioned No.
167. Like others of its type, it was
destined to be replaced by a vehicle
much more economical to operate and
maintain—the bus.

A reminder of a bygone time when
trains of its ilk were a familiar sight in
the Bay Area, OBRT No. 167 now
spends its days among the more than
200 streetcars, locomotives, coaches,
interurbans, and other types of rolling
stock at the Orange Empire Rail
Museum in Perris, California.

1960
Metro-North Commuter Railroad
No. 2024

General Motors EMD (Bo-A1A)
Class FL-9 Electro-Diesel Passenger
Locomotive

A unique solution to the problem of running a diesel locomotive into New York City (whose laws prohibited operation of locos that emitted fumes), the electro-diesel FL-9 was created especially for the New Haven Railroad at a time when the line was considering switching from electric to diesel operations.

General Motors EMD modified a standard FP-9 cab unit to operate on electric power when required and added a three-axle trailing truck to comply with axleload restrictions (creating a new Bo-A1A wheel arrangement). Sixty of these unusual engines were built for the New Haven between 1956 and 1960.

Originally appearing in the New Haven's red, white, and black "McGinnis" colors of the period when built in 1960, No. 2024 was later transferred to the Metro-North Commuter Railroad, which began operating on former New Haven trackage in the 1980s. Numerous FL-9s continue to operate in the New York City metropolitan area—still wearing their New Haven colors to commemorate that late, great line.

1960

1960-1969

While much of the nation's freight is still hauled by powerful diesels with nicknames like "U-boats" and "Geeps," air travel all but kills America's passenger rail business—and with it, such once-mighty lines as the B&O, the Pennsy, and the New York Central.

1961
Baltimore & Ohio Railroad No. 1961
Daylight Speedliner

Budd Company Rail Diesel Car
(RDC-2) Baggage/Diner/Coach

Leave it to two of the most innovative organizations in railroading history—the Baltimore & Ohio Railroad and the Budd Manufacturing Company—to develop what still ranks among the most unique self-propelled cars ever to ride America's rails.

The Budd Company began building distinctive streamliners with 1934's *Zephyr*. Fifteen years later it introduced the legendary product simply referred to as the "Budd car": the Rail Diesel Car (RDC). A lightweight, stainless-steel "pocket streamliner" with diesel engines and transmissions beneath its floor, the RDC was used primarily in commuter or shortline service—until the B&O decided to try something different. Between 1956 and 1963, "America's first railroad"

operated the unique *Daylight Speedliner* service from the East Coast to Pittsburgh. Its specially built Budd RDC-2s were the first ever used in long-distance service and included the *Speedliner* car shown here at the B&O Museum: B&O No. 1961, one of only two baggage/diner/coach RDCs ever made.

1962
Delaware & Hudson
Railway No. 413

Alco C-420 (Bo-Bo) 2000-hp
Diesel-Electric Switching Locomotive

After reigning among the greatest producers of steam locomotives in history, the legendary American Locomotive Company (Alco) had also broken ground in the diesel-electric arena with its original 1000-hp RS-1 in 1941. In the early 1960s, Alco finally took that innovative road switcher off the roster, after a remarkable 19-year run alongside many later RS models. Its successor was the 2000-hp C-420, the first in a new series of Century road switchers unveiled in 1962.

The "C" in the C-420's model number stands for "Century" (instead of denoting a three-axle truck as usual), while the "4" indicates a four-wheel truck, and "20" refers to the horsepower divided by 100. Distinguished from the earlier RS designs by its low nose and pointed cab, the C-420 is represented here by Delaware & Hudson No. 413, which ran on the line's 734 miles of trackage in New York, Pennsylvania, and Vermont to eastern Canada.

1963
New York Central
Railroad No. 4096

General Motors EMD (A1A-A1A)
Class E-9A Diesel-Electric
Locomotive

Like many great locomotives now
residing in museums, No. 4096
narrowly escaped the scrap heap after
a colorful and historic career on the
rails. Originally a 2400-hp E-9A built
for the Union Pacific in December
1963, it was in fact the third from last
of the fabled E-series locomotives
produced by EMD's La Grange plant.
As UP No. 912A, it hauled the line's
final westbound passenger run from
Chicago in April 1971.

Sold a few years later to the newly
formed Amtrak and rebuilt as 2600-hp
No. 417, this E-9A really got around;
it was leased to the MBTA for
Boston-area commuter service, as well

as to the Auto-Train Corporation, for which it pulled the very last run in April 1981. Rescued in 1985 by the Connecticut Valley Railroad Museum and restored as the fictitious New York Central No. 4096, it is now privately owned and on loan to the Danbury Rail Museum.

1964
Baltimore & Ohio
Railroad No. 7402

General Motors EMD (Co-Co) SD-35
Diesel-Electric Freight Locomotive

Satisfying the needs of railroads
where climatic conditions demanded
greater adhesion than even the tough
GP-series general-purpose locomotives
could deliver, General Motors created
the six-axle SD ("special duty") series
to complement its mighty "Geeps" in
the early 1950s. Introduced in 1964,
the SD-35 was the 2500-hp entry in
EMD's SD lineup. Although outsold
nearly 4 to 1 by the SD-40, its larger

3000-hp sister, over 300 SD-35's
labored for railroads large and small,
along with a handful of SDP-35
variants equipped for passenger
service.

This particular SD-35 was built in
1964 as Baltimore & Ohio No. 7402,
later becoming CSXT No. 4550 after
B&O's absorption into the Chessie
system. Retiring in 1993 following
nearly 30 years of service, this workhorse was refurbished and restored to
its original B&O livery and number at
the B&O Railroad Museum, where it
can be seen today.

1965
Maine Central
Railroad No. 228

General Electric (Bo-Bo) U-25B
Diesel-Electric Locomotive

Commonly referred to by railfans as
"U-boats," General Electric
Corporation's Universal series of road
switchers marked the corporate
giant's entry into complete locomotive
production after more than a half-
century of experience building electric
components and systems for other
locomotive manufacturers.

Between 1940 and 1953, GE had
served as the American Locomotive
Company's exclusive, noncompeting
supplier of electrical systems. But with
Alco struggling in the early 1950s, GE
terminated this agreement and soon
plunged into developing motive power
of its own design. The first of the GE
diesels was the four-axle, 2500-hp
U-25B, which debuted in 1960 as the
most powerful locomotive then on the
U.S. market.

GE built and sold an impressive 478
U-25Bs between 1959 and 1966, along
with more than 100 units of the loco-
motive's later six-axled version, the
U-25C. Manufactured in 1965, the
U-25B seen here became Maine
Central No. 228, after earlier service
with the Midwest's storied Rock
Island Line.

1966
Baltimore & Ohio
Railroad No. 3684

General Motors EMD (Bo-Bo) GP-40
Diesel-Electric Freight Locomotive

Enjoying the lion's share of sales in
virtually every variety of diesel-electric
locomotive produced right through the
1960s, General Motors' EMD introduced yet another "Geep" to the fold
in 1965: the 3000-hp GP-40. Two
successive (and successful) versions
of this mighty hauler—the GP-40
(produced until 1971) and the GP-40-2
or Dash-2 (built between 1972 and
1986)—helped EMD to continue its
dominance in the diesel market for
decades.

The first of its type built for and
delivered to the Baltimore & Ohio
for freight duties in 1966, GP-40
No. 3684 was renumbered as CSXT
No. 6500 after completing three
decades' active service. In 1994, it was
repainted to its original appearance for
display at Baltimore's B&O Museum.

1967
Lackawanna Valley
Railroad No. 901

General Electric (Bo-Bo) U-30B
Diesel-Electric Locomotive

Upping the ante in its ongoing horsepower race with competitors Alco
and GM's EMD, General Electric
developed progressively more powerful versions of its "U-boat" diesel road
switchers in the mid-1960s. From its
original 2500-hp U-25B introduced
earlier in the decade (see 1965), GE
cranked things up by bringing out the
2800-hp U-28B in 1966, then pushed
them even further later that year with
the 3000-hp U-30B. This successful
design would stay in production
through 1975, even as GE developed
other Universal-series switchers with
3300- and 3600-hp ratings.

Although early units were barely
distinguishable from some of their
U-28B cousins, later U-30Bs featured
a snub nose and fairly distinctive
radiator patterns. The one shown
here, manufactured in 1967, rendered
service for the New York Central
before assuming its current identity as
Lackawanna Valley No. 901.

1968   New York, Susquehanna & Western Railway No. 3000

Alco C-430 (Bo-Bo) 3000-hp
Diesel-Electric Switching Locomotive

With its bold yellow-and-black livery
standing vividly against a clear blue
sky, NYS&W No. 3000 represents
the final efforts of the once-great
American Locomotive Company to
compete with General Motors and
General Electric for a piece of the
four-axle road switcher market—the

Alco C-430. Although a number of
them are still on the rails today, only
about 16 of these 3000-hp Century-
series locomotives were produced
(between 1966 and 1968), and they
were unable to help Alco regain a
competitive edge.

In 1968, the last ten C-430s were
purchased by the New York Central
Railroad, and they were, in fact, the

1969 Monongohela Connecting Railroad No. 701

Alco C-415 (Bo-Bo) 1500-hp Diesel-Electric Switching Locomotive

For 120 straight years, locomotives rolled out of a plant on the Erie Canal in Schenectady, New York, known as the "Big Shop." Begun in 1848 as the Schenectady Locomotive Engine Manufactory, it was one of eight works that merged in 1901 to form the American Locomotive Company, popularly (and, later, officially) called Alco.

As the Big Shop marked its centennial in 1948, Alco—after building 75,000 steam locomotives—halted its steam operations to focus on diesel production. But two decades later, withering competition from General Motors and General Electric forced Alco to succumb; in 1969, the Big Shop closed its doors for good.

One of the last locos to roll out of an Alco plant (in July 1968), No. 701 is also unique—the only 1500-hp C-415 with an optional tight-clearance cab. After a career spent switching cars in Pittsburgh steel mills for the Monongohela Connecting Railroad, it now resides at Strasburg's Railroad Museum of Pennsylvania.

final locomotives delivered to the line before it merged with the Pennsy into the short-lived Penn Central. C-430 No. 3000 was photographed 22 years later, hard at work for the New York, Susquehanna & Western Railway, whose advertising urged potential customers to "Ship with Susie-Q."

1970
Consolidated Rail
Corporation
(Conrail) No. 6905
and No. 6908

General Electric (Co-Co) U-23C
Diesel-Electric Locomotives

These "twin sisters" in Conrail livery
are two of about 20 or so General
Electric U-23Cs still in operation, out
of a total of 53 manufactured between
1968 and 1970. The U-23C was a
six-axle (Co-Co) version of GE's
intermediate "U-boat" diesel road
switcher, the U-23B (see 1972). Both
units were powered by a 12-cylinder
version of GE's standard diesel engine
and produced either 2250 or 2300
horsepower. The fact that nearly
half of all U-23Cs (and about three-
quarters of all U-23Bs) are still on the
rails today—nearly 30 years later—
attests to the locomotive's reliability.

This photo of Conrail No. 6905 and
No. 6908 sitting side by side was
taken a quarter-century after both
locomotives rolled out of the GE
plant in 1970. At the time they were
built, Conrail itself was still about
six years away. A Philadelphia-based
consolidation of six bankrupt eastern
railroads, Conrail began operations
in 1976.

1970-1979

After the demise of Alco in the sixties, General Motors and General Electric dominate the diesel locomotive market. With many of America's lines in turmoil, Amtrak and Conrail are created—and an electric train from France becomes the world's fastest.

1971
Consolidated Rail Corporation (Conrail) No. 7896

General Motors EMD (Bo-Bo) GP-38
Diesel-Electric Freight Locomotive

Following up on the successful debut of the 3000-hp GP-40 locomotive in 1965, General Motors EMD guessed that the market also had room for a hauler with slightly less horsepower, and the GP-38 proved them right. A high-hooded, versatile 2000-hp "Geep" designed to run hard and long, the GP-38 turned out to be just what many railroads needed. It sold so well during its initial production run—over 700 units between 1966 and 1971—that EMD launched an even more successful GP-38-2 in 1972. All told,

nearly 3000 GP-38s and GP-38-2s went into service on lines throughout the United States and Canada, and many are still in there kicking. One of them is shown here wearing vivid Conrail blue in 1993: Locomotive No. 7896, a GP-38 built toward the end of the production run in 1970.

1972
Canadian Pacific Railway (CP Rail) No. 5425

General Motors EMD (Co-Co)
SD-40-2 Diesel-Electric Freight
Locomotive

If you've ever wondered what's the most common locomotive in North America, stop wondering—you're looking at it! It's General Motors' incredibly successful SD-40-2—a six-axle, 3000-hp freight hauler powered by EMD's 16-cylinder 645-E3 diesel engine. Launched in 1972 as a successor to the popular SD-40 (built between 1966 and 1972), the SD-40-2 continued to roll off the EMD assembly lines through 1986. By that time nearly 4000 of these second-generation "special duty" diesels had been put into service on railways throughout North America, where they are a frequent sight even today.

With its bright-yellow livery caught in the floodlights used to pierce the blackness of night, this particular SD-40-2—Canadian Pacific Railway No. 5425, built in 1974 and seen here photographed in 1997—makes a mighty majestic picture of modern locomotive power.

1973
Delaware & Hudson Railway No. 7418

General Motors EMD (Bo-Bo)
GP-39-2 Diesel-Electric Locomotive

When EMD brought the 2300-hp GP-39 to market in 1969, the division offered the turbocharged 12-cylinder "Geep" as an alternative to—and perhaps a replacement for—the nearly identical 16-cylinder, 2000-hp GP-38 introduced three years earlier. However, most railroads preferred to avoid the high cost of maintaining turbochargers and stayed away from the GP-39 in droves. Only 23 were built, and by 1972 the model had been removed from the EMD catalog. In the meantime, the earlier GP-38 really caught on, and a second

version, the GP-38-2, went on to phenomenal success.

But strangely enough, that wasn't the end of the GP-39 story. In 1973, the worldwide "oil crisis" made fuel economy a priority—and suddenly the turbocharged 12-cylinder engine looked like a pretty good idea. The "new" model was put into production as the GP-39-2; nearly 250 were built through 1987. The example shown here, Delaware & Hudson No. 7418, is a GP-39-2 from 1973.

1974
Reading & Northern Railroad No. 2399

General Electric (Bo-Bo) U-23B
Diesel-Electric Locomotive

In the late 1960s, General Electric watched closely as General Motors EMD scored big with both the intermediate 2000-hp GP-38 (see 1971) and the high-powered 3000-hp GP-40. To answer this two-pronged attack, GE opted for a lower-powered "U-boat" whose 12-cylinder engine was less expensive to maintain than the standard 16-cylinder powerplant.

It wasn't long before the result, the 2250-hp U-23B, paid off. Sales were brisk, and approximately 425 were built before the run ended in 1977. But it wasn't until the hauler had been in use for several years before its most remarkable trait—amazing durability— became apparent to the industry.

The equipment rosters of many North American railroads indicate that close to 75 percent of the U-23Bs produced by GE—all now between 20 and 30 years old—are still operational today. Among them is Reading & Northern No. 2399, a U-23B of 1974 vintage, seen here on the road in 1997.

1975

STOURBRIDGE

1975 Stourbridge Railroad No. 44

General Motors EMD/AT&SF Shops (Bo-Bo) CF-7 Diesel-Electric Road Switcher

At first glance, this bright-yellow road switcher trundling through a snow-covered field may look like just another among thousands of slightly varying freight haulers built by industry giant General Motors EMD since the mid-1960s. But the colorful history of this unique EMD locomotive, the 1500-hp CF-7, is a bit more complicated than most, and in fact starts back in the early 1950s.

Like every CF-7, this general-purpose road switcher began life two decades earlier as a classic EMD F-7A freight locomotive (see 1950) built between 1949 and 1953 for the historic Atchison, Topeka & Santa Fe Railroad. In a massive rebuilding program from 1970 through 1978, the AT&SF's shops in Cleburne, Texas, used new "Geep" hoods, underframes, and other parts to transform 233 tired F-7As into gleaming new CF-7s. After years with the Santa Fe, many CF-7s now haul freight on short lines across the country—like No. 44, photographed at work for Pennsylvania's Stourbridge Railroad on a bright winter's day in 1992.

1976
Florida East Coast
Railway (FEC)
No. 501

General Motors EMD (Bo-Bo)
GP-38-2 Diesel-Electric
Freight Locomotive

The second version of EMD's trusty
GP-38 diesel, the 2000-hp GP-38-2,
proved to be even more popular
with America's railroads than the
model's earlier incarnation. While a
respectable 730 GP-38s were
purchased during five years of
production (1965–1971), the Dash-2
far outsold its predecessor; nearly
2200 were built between 1972 and
1984. Both versions of this durable
16-cylinder "Geep" were nearly
identical. The major difference was in
the electronics, which on the GP-38-2
were housed in a modular cabinet system. The Dash-2 readily found a niche
with main- and short-line roads alike,
and many are still in service today.

The 1977-built GP-38-2 shown here,
No. 501, was photographed hauling
freight in 1986 for the historic Florida
East Coast Railway. Established in
the 1880s, the FEC once ran out to
the Florida Keys, but hurricanes later
forced abandonment of that trackage,
which now serves as a highway.

1977
Boston & Maine
Railroad No. 314

General Motors EMD (Bo-Bo)
GP-40-2 Diesel-Electric
Freight Locomotive

Distinguished from their 2000-hp GP-
38 cousins by three large radiator fans

and a turbocharger stack on their
hoods, EMD's 3000-hp GP-40 series
locomotives enabled General Motors
to carve out an even bigger slice of the
diesel market through the 1970s and
1980s.

Here's an example of the GP-40-2, the
second version of the type, launched
in 1972 and produced in a quantity of
about 1100 through 1986. The only
distinctive outward difference between
the models is the battery-box cover,
which on the Dash 2 is bolted instead
of hinged. The GP-40-2 seen trackside
in this 1989 photograph, Boston &
Maine No. 314, features a rubber-
sprung Blomberg M truck. It was
among 18 brand-spanking-new 3000-
hp EMD locomotives bought by the
B&M in 1977.

The merger of several earlier Massachusetts lines created the venerable
Boston & Maine in 1842. The system,
comprising 1400 miles of trackage,
continues to serve New England
today.

1978
Consolidated Rail
Corporation
(Conrail) No. 1983

General Electric (Bo-Bo) B-23-7
Diesel-Electric Switching Locomotive

This photo of a General Electric
B-23-7, Conrail No. 1983, under
power was taken in 1999—more than
two decades after the 2250-hp road
switcher first hit the rails in 1978.
Designed to replace the Universal (or
"U-boat") series U-23B as part of the
new "Dash 7" line, the durable B-23-7
debuted in 1977 and stayed in GE's
catalog until 1984. Approximately 536
were sold.

Rugged road switchers like the B-23-7
have been the mainstay of Conrail's
operations since it opened for business
in 1976. Based in Philadelphia, the
Consolidated Rail Corporation began
as a government-invested operation
of six bankrupt lines—the Central
of New Jersey, Lehigh & Hudson
River, Reading, Lehigh Valley, Erie
Lackawanna, and Penn Central.
It went public in 1987 and in 1999
began operating under joint control of
CSXT and Norfolk Southern.

1979
SNCF (French National Railways) TGV

Alsthom High-Speed Articulated
Electric Passenger Train

The attainment of higher speeds has
been a major concern in virtually all
transportation technologies throughout this century, and railroads are
no exception. Since the steam age,
locomotive designers have striven to
propel passengers and freight faster
than before.

In Europe, electric motive power has
been employed for decades to whisk
passengers at record speeds, and the
French company Alsthom has been
a major player in the development
of high-speed electric trains since
mid-century. After two experimental
French electrics exceeded 200 mph
in tests in 1955, the industry moved
gradually toward producing a train
that could top 150 mph in normal
passenger operations.

The result was Alsthom's TGV *(Train
à Grande Vitesse),* an articulated
electric trainset that began operations
on SNCF's Paris-Lyons line in the
late 1970s. Originally designed with a
gas turbine (but electrified after the
1973 oil crisis), the TGV operates at
close to 170 mph. In 1981, one set a
new world record of 236 mph. This
1999 photo, taken at the railroad
station in Perpignan, France, features
TGV No. 4528.

1980
Florida East Coast
Railway (FEC)
No. 445

General Motors EMD (Bo-Bo)
GP-40-3 Diesel-Electric
Freight Locomotive

Recently celebrating its centennial in 1995, the Florida East Coast Railway is the Sunshine State's only railroad still operating under the same name for that long a stretch. In the 1880s, Standard Oil partner Henry M. Flagler bought the tiny Jacksonville, St. Augustine & Halifax River Railway while developing a tourist empire on Florida's Atlantic coast, and from it he built the FEC. Once stretching all the way out to Key West, this historic line still endures after a century beset by bankruptcy, protracted labor violence, and frequently deadly hurricanes.

Today's FEC operates as a freight service along the Florida coast between Jacksonville and Miami, hauling such commodities as crushed stone and other building supplies, trailer and container flatcars, and basic consumer goods.

For its centennial, the line rebuilt three 3000-hp EMD diesels into special 100th Anniversary GP-40-3 units, numbered 445 to 447 and bearing the slogan "Speedway to America's Playground." The one shown here, FEC No. 445, was originally built in 1980.

1980-1989

Horsepower seems to climb with the introduction of each new diesel hauler, and the nation's freight moves at an ever-increasing rate. As ridership of suburban commuter trains grows, innovative technology still strives for increased speed and comfort.

1981
New Jersey Transit No. 4129

General Motors EMD (Bo-Bo)
F-40-PH Diesel-Electric Locomotive

A sloped nose, short full-width hood, and lack of a front platform are a few of the distinguishing features of EMD's F-40-PH, a 3000-hp "cowl-unit" locomotive designed with short-haul passenger and commuter service in mind.

Introduced in 1976, the F-40-PH was built with a 500-kilowatt alternator providing head-end electrical power (rather than steam) for heating and lighting passenger cars. Amtrak put the first F-40-PHs into service, upgrading the alternator and adding a fuel tank to those units destined to become the prime movers for the road's Superliner trains.

In production through 1988, this semi-streamlined passenger hauler was soon adopted by many suburban lines throughout North America and is commonly seen pulling (or pushing)

commuter trains in and around such cities as Chicago, New York, Boston, San Francisco, and Toronto. This 1998 photograph features New Jersey Transit No. 4129, an F-40-PH manufactured by General Motors in 1981.

1982
Amtrak (National Railroad Passenger Corporation) No. 953

General Motors EMD/ASEA (Bo-Bo)
AEM-7 Electric Passenger
Locomotive

Whizzing along at speeds of up to 125 mph, the double-ended AEM-7 electric boxcab—dubbed the "Toaster" by rail-fans—is one of the fastest locomotives in North America. A cooperative effort between General Motors EMD, Sweden's ASEA (who designed and licensed it), and the Budd Company (who built the carbody), the AEM-7 joined Amtrak's roster in 1980. Since then it has hauled the national passenger line's fast Metroliner service along the electrified trackage between Washington, DC, and New Haven, Connecticut.

Putting out a whopping 7000 hp, the AEM-7 replaced the ancient GG-1 electrics that initially ran the Northeast Corridor for Amtrak, which began operating the nation's intercity rail passenger service in 1971. The AEM-7 (signifying ASEA, EMD, and the 7000-hp rating) also performs commuter duties in several metropolitan areas. Amtrak No. 953, shown here on the road in 1999, was among Amtrak's third shipment of new AEM-7s taken in 1982.

**General Motors EMD (Co-Co)
SD-50-2 Diesel-Electric
Freight Locomotive**

It takes a trained eye to tell an SD-50 from an SD-60, but both of these behemoths are more powerful follow-ups to EMD's wildly successful six-axle, 3000-hp SD-40 freight hauler. The 3500-hp SD-50, built between 1981 and 1985, features six door panels beneath its radiator inlet grilles, four of which have latches. That's basically the only outward difference between it and the 3800-hp SD-60 (in production from 1984 to 1981), which has six latched doors out of a total of eight. (And you'd better count those doors pretty fast!)

Conrail purchased a whopping 140 SD-50 or SD-50-2 units for its freight operations throughout the eastern

United States. Some of those, including a group numbered 6700 to 6739, employed Flexicoil-type trucks, although most SD-50s were produced with trucks of the high-traction type. One of that number—Conrail No. 6702, delivered in 1983—is shown here on the rails a dozen years later.

1984
Consolidated Rail Corporation (Conrail) No. 6563

**General Electric (Co-Co) C-30-7
Diesel-Electric Locomotive**

Because so many of the diesels in these pages were produced by General

Motors EMD, it may appear that GM completely dominated the locomotive market in the 1980s. But General Electric had also long enjoyed a sizable share of the diesel market, and eventually took first place in locomotive sales—thanks in great measure to the success of the reliable C-30-7 (Dash-7) series of freight haulers.

Resembling GE's earlier "U-boat" locos from which it evolved, the 3000-hp C-30-7 first appeared in 1976 and remained in production through 1985. Of the more than 1100 units sold in the United States and Mexico, over a thousand are still hard at work today. The locomotive's main identifying feature—part of the hood that widens at a "break" just behind the power assembly doors—can be seen in this head-on photo of Conrail No. 6563, a C-30-7 built in 1984.

1985
Canadian Pacific Railway (CP Rail) No. 3057

General Motors EMD (Bo-Bo)
GP-38-2 Diesel-Electric
Freight Locomotive

In a classic winter scene sure to warm the heart of North American railfans (especially those partial to the venerable Canadian Pacific Railway), CP Rail No. 3057 trundles across a snowy landscape in 1996. A fine example of one of EMD's most successful locomotives ever, this particular GP-38-2 was built in late 1985, one of 115 later models produced for Canadian Pacific between 1983 and 1987 that featured the free-flow blower duct introduced in 1982 (visible on the side, aft of the numbered cab).

A revised version of EMD's trusty GP-38 diesel, the 2000-hp GP-38-2 debuted in 1972 and enjoyed a remarkable 15-year production run. A total of 2188 units of this reliable, versatile "Geep" were put into service: 1801 in the United States, 133 in Mexico, and 254 (including the one shown here) in Canada. Many of them are still chugging merrily along the rails as you read this.

1986
Florida East Coast
Railway (FEC)
No. 434

General Motors EMD (Bo-Bo)
GP-40-2 Diesel-Electric
Freight Locomotive

Sure, it makes a pretty picture crossing one of coastal Florida's innumerable bridges in this photograph, but that's not the only reason why Florida East Coast Railway No. 434 is featured here. Although still hard at work at its "day job" for FEC, it is also a historic diesel locomotive—the very last GP-40-2 ever built by General Motors Electro-Motive Division.

The 3000-hp GP-40 and GP-40-2 (see 1977) were among EMD's most successful locomotives, extremely popular with America's freight railroads. Taken together, more than 2300 of the two models were produced over 21 years. The second series, the GP-40-2, debuted in 1972 and remained in production for 14 years. The 1121st and last rolled out of EMD's La Grange plant in 1986—and you're looking at it now, still hauling all manner of goods up and down the Florida coast.

1987
Consolidated Rail
Corporation
(Conrail) No. 5024

General Electric (Bo-Bo) B-36-7
Diesel-Electric Switching Locomotive

The locomotives of General Electric's Dash-7 series are similar to the Universal ("U-boat") line they were designed to replace, with one distinctive major feature: the "step" in the hood just forward of the exhaust stack. This 3600-hp B-36-7—Conrail No. 5024, built in 1983—is typical of the Dash-7 diesels that first appeared in 1977 and soon became a fixture on trackage operated by the Consolidated Rail Corporation (Conrail).

Created in 1976 from the ashes of the bankrupt Jersey Central, Lehigh & Hudson, Reading, Lehigh Valley, Erie Lackawanna and Penn Central, Conrail was the Government's attempt to prevent the collapse of America's freight railroads. Initially using Federal funds to revitalize its vast network, the line finally turned a profit in 1981. On March 26, 1987, Conrail went public, thereby returning the East's rail freight system to the private sector. It was purchased jointly a dozen years later by CSXT and Norfolk Southern.

1988
Tri-Rail No. 805

General Motors EMD/Morrison-Knudsen (Bo-Bo) F-40-PHL-2 Diesel-Electric Locomotive

An interesting example of the many hybrid locomotives built (or, in this case, rebuilt) to suit the particular needs of commuter railroads, the F-40-PHL-2 seen here is a modification of EMD's 3000-hp F-40-PH passenger locomotive produced through 1988. In 1987 the Boise, Idaho, contract rebuilding firm of Morrison-Knudsen rebuilt five F-40-PH hood units with FP-series cabs to create the unique 3200-hp F-40-PHL-2 locomotive. The "L" in the model number most likely indicates that this variant is longer (by 3 feet) than the standard F-40-PH.

All five of these unusual switchers were manufactured to push and pull double-decker passenger trains for Tri-Rail, Southern Florida's commuter rail system linking the Palm Beach, Fort Lauderdale, and Miami metropolitan areas. The one shown here toiling under a blue Florida sky in 1996, Tri-Rail No. 805, was rebuilt from a locomotive originally manufactured in 1968.

1989
Consolidated Rail Corporation (Conrail) No. 6042

General Electric (Co-Co) C-40-8 (Dash 8-40C) Diesel-Electric Locomotive

As the 1980s drew to a close, General Electric landed at the top of the diesel locomotive heap, thanks in large measure to the success of the 4000-hp Dash 8, which debuted in 1987 and was eventually manufactured in three body styles. The C-40-8 version represented here by Conrail No. 6042, built in 1989, is still available today. The wide-nosed C-40-8-W (see 1991) was produced from 1989 to 1995, and the Draper-body Canadian variant, the C-40-8-M, was produced from 1990 to 1994.

Although sold in fewer numbers than its wide-nosed W version (655 units to date, as compared to 875), the C-40-8 proved popular with freight lines, and it is a common sight on American trackage. However, like many modern diesels, it doesn't exactly stand out in a crowd. Nearly identical to the C-39-8-E, it can be discerned by a "breakless" hood flush with the cab, a notched fuel tank with two air reservoirs, and side-by-side headlights.

1990
Metro-North
New Haven Line

Multiple-Unit (M.U.) Electric
Commuter Passenger Railcar

As the 1990s began, commuter
railroads of major American cities
struggled to maintain consistent levels
of service, often with trackage and
equipment from numerous failed lines.
Among them is the Metro-North
Commuter Railroad, run jointly by
New York City's Metropolitan
Transit Authority and the State of
Connecticut, comprising parts of the
fabled New York, New Haven &
Hartford, and New York Central
Railroads.

Metro-North's New Haven Line is
unique because it operates with two
types of electric delivery systems along
different parts of the line. One stretch
consists of a third rail delivering 600
volts of direct current (DC), with
shoes that slide beneath the rail, and
the other consists of an overhead wire
that supplies 13,000 volts of alternating current (AC). Since its birth in
1982, Metro-North has operated
an assortment of equipment, from
traditional Budd stainless-steel cars to
the latest electric M.U. (multiple-unit)
cars built in Japan.

1990-2000

As the "American Century"—
a time whose remarkable
progress owes much to the
nation's railroads—draws to a
close, old trains soldier on, while
high-speed trains in Europe, Asia,
and the United States offer a
glimpse of rail technology for the
next century and beyond.

1991
Consolidated Rail Corporation (Conrail) No. 6151

General Electric (Co-Co) C-40-8-W
(Dash 8-40CW)
Diesel-Electric Locomotive

Whether you call it by its popular name, "Dash 8-40CW," or by General Electric's official designation of "C-40-8-W," this wide-cab, microprocessor-controlled diesel has spearheaded GE's drive to supremacy in the locomotive market of the 1990s. Following up its successful Dash 7 series of freight haulers with the Dash 8s in the second half of the 1980s, GE barreled headlong into the new decade with several variations of the series' hardy 4000-hp entry, the C-40-8.

The most popular variant, the C-40-8-W seen here, employs a wide-nosed cab with its corners dropped (to allow the crew in the cab to see who is standing on the steps). In production from 1989 to 1995 (and still occasionally built to order), it is a symbol of modern railroading, with about 875 units on the rails today—as witnessed by this 1999 photo of Conrail No. 6151, a C-40-8-W built in 1991.

1992
Soo Line No. 6059

General Motors EMD (Co-Co)
SD-60-M Diesel-Electric
Freight Locomotive

In the confusing world of modern diesel locomotives, it's not surprising that it's easier to tell the difference between an SD-60-M and an SD-60 than to tell that same SD-60 from an SD-50! How? By a nose!

While the 3800-hp SD-60 is virtually identical to the 3500-hp SD-50, the wide nose of the SD-60-M (the "North American Cab") makes it easy to distinguish from the standard SD-60. More than 500 SD-60-Ms have been built since EMD introduced the model in 1989. Soo Line purchased five, including No. 6059, seen in a dramatic night photo taken in 1992, the year of its manufacture.

The midwestern Soo Line was created by the 1961 merger of the Minneapolis, St. Paul & Sault Ste. Marie; the Wisconsin Central; and the Duluth, South Shore & Atlantic. Currently controlled by Canadian Pacific Railway, the 4500-plus-mile system derives its name from the proper pronunciation of "Sault" in "Sault Ste. Marie."

1994
Canadian Pacific
Railway (CP Rail)
No. 1828

Montreal Locomotive Works
RS-18-R (Bo-Bo) Diesel-Electric
Switching Locomotive

The fact that late-model diesel locomotives from General Electric and General Motors EMD dominate the North American rails doesn't mean that old workhorses built and/or designed decades ago by a former champion—Alco—can't still pull their weight. And CP Rail No. 1828, an RS-18-2 built in 1958, is living proof, as this 1994 photograph shows.

Produced by Montreal Locomotive Works between 1956 and 1968, the

1993
Durango &
Silverton Narrow-
Gauge Railroad
No. 480

Baldwin 2-8-2 (Mikado)
Narrow-Gauge Steam Locomotive

Lest you think that only computer-controlled modern diesels are propelling passengers in the 1990s, we present a blast from the past: honest-to-goodness steam power, courtesy of the Durango & Silverton Narrow-Gauge Railroad! One of many tourist railroads offering riders a trip back in time, the Durango & Silverton is the "real McCoy"—a year-round steam passenger operation along historic trackage through Colorado's breathtaking San Juan National Forest. Originally part of the Denver & Rio Grande Railway, the line was built in the 1880s to haul precious metals out of the San Juan Mountains, but it has carried passengers on scenic excursions from its earliest days.

The Durango & Silverton's roster includes vintage rolling stock and

narrow-gauge steam locomotives from the 1920s and 1930s. In this 1993 photo, steam billows from D&S No. 480—a narrow-gauge, Baldwin-built 1925 Mikado—as passengers alight from car No. 213, a classic coach from bygone days.

1800-hp RS-18 was the Canadian version of Alco's RS-11 and RS-36 series. Early examples employed a hood style that made the RS-18 virtually indistinguishable from the 1600-hp RS-10 (also a Canada-only design). Later units, however, like the RS-18-2 seen here hard at work for CP Rail at the ripe old age of 36, had a modified long hood and "chopped" nose.

1995　New Hope & Ivyland Railroad No. 1513

Alco RSC-2 (A1A-A1A)
Diesel-Electric Switching Locomotive

When one sees the relatively ancient diesel locomotive pictured here trundle by, one can almost hear a variation of that old Army song: "And the Alcos keep rolling along." Although the American Locomotive Company ceased production in 1969, many of its diesels—descendants of the first true road switcher, the RS-1 (see 1942 and 1948)—were still at work decades later. And here's a prime example: New Hope & Ivyland Railroad No. 1513, an Alco RSC-2 chugging along nearly a half-century after it was built in 1949.

A six-wheel variant of Alco's versatile RS-2, the 1500- or 1600-hp RSC-2 was produced in limited quantities between 1946 and 1950, and it handled passenger and freight duties admirably for many years. Although some spotters' guides indicate that the RSC-2 has virtually disappeared from America's rails, this one was photographed hauling passengers for the NH&I's Pennsylvania tourist operations near the Delaware Canal in 1995.

1996
Amtrak
(National Railroad
Passenger
Corporation)
No. 700

General Electric (Bo-Bo) AMD-110
Genesis (P-32-AC-DM)
Diesel-Electric Passenger Locomotive

The old adage about "the old becomes
new again" could apply to modern
passenger locomotive design. Six
decades after the streamlined steam
engines of the 1930s—and four
since the sleek diesels of the 1950s—
streamlining is back in the 1990s, on
Amtrak's unique Genesis passenger
diesel.

Representing a fresh approach to
locomotive design, this sleek diesel
was originally produced by General
Electric in 1993 in a 4000-hp version
called either AMD-103 (for "Amtrak
Diesel 103 mph") or "P-40." It was
later named "Genesis" in a promotional contest. With its flush-fitted,
slant-nosed body that resembles an
inchworm to some, it makes quite an
impression at the head of Amtrak and
Metro-North passenger trains.

The Genesis shown here, Amtrak
No. 700, is an AMD-110 (or
P-32-AC-DM). It is the "Phase II,"
3200-hp, third-rail (diesel and electric)
version introduced in 1996 to operate
in and out of New York's Penn
Station.

General Motors EMD (Co-Co)
SD-80-MAC Diesel-Electric
Freight Locomotive

After losing its lead in the diesel locomotive market to General Electric in
the 1980s, General Motors EMD
hoped to regain its footing in the 1990s

with a powerful line of "Special Duty" freight haulers employing new radial trucks and innovative AC (alternating current) traction motors by Siemens Transportation Systems. Launched with the experimental SD-60-MAC in 1991 and the SD-70-MAC in 1993, the series (dubbed the "Big Mac" line) featured EMD's wide-nosed North American Cab and many other features common to the earlier SD-60-M and SD-70-M locomotives.

Longer (with a total length of 80 feet, 2 inches) and more powerful (by 1000 hp) than the SD-70-MAC, the 5000-hp SD-80-MAC debuted in the mid-nineties and is distinguishable from its other SD cousins through its protruding, canted radiator assembly. SD-80-MACs like this one—Conrail No. 4122, built in 1997 and photographed at work in 1999—represent the future of diesel freight power on America's rails.

1998
Middletown &
Hummelstown
Railroad No. 1016

Alco T-6 (Bo-Bo) 1000-hp
Diesel-Electric Switching Locomotive

As the 1990s roll on and the end of
the twentieth century approaches,
North America's mainline railroads
feature ever-more-powerful, ever-
more-sophisticated motive power from
General Electric and General Motors
EMD. But for scores of little "short-
line" operations, secondhand, decades-
old locomotives are (and always have
been) the order of the day—still
rendering yeoman's service on freight
runs throughout "small-town
America."

Witness the colorful end-cab diesel
switcher shown here, Middlestown &
Hummelstown Railroad No. 1016.

A hardy example of Alco's T-6—a
1000-hp "transfer" switcher that
debuted in 1958—it was built in 1969,
the last year of operation for what
was once the world's largest locomotive plant. Nearly thirty years later,
on a wintry day in 1998, it was
photographed hauling a line of
tankers for Pennsylvania's M&H,
a former Reading System short line
running independent freight and
tourist operations since 1976.

1999
Delaware-
Lackawanna
Railroad No. 310

Alco C-420 (Bo-Bo) 2000-hp
Diesel-Electric Switching Locomotive

Before looking forward to the year
2000 and a new millennium, we
have chosen to mark the twentieth
century's last year by literally looking
back at a "Century" still going strong:
a C-420, the first of Alco's Century
series of road switchers introduced in
the 1960s (see 1962). Although the
Schenectady shop that produced it—
at one time the world's largest—has
been closed for 30 years, this Alco
hauler and others like it continue to
serve the industry faithfully and well
in 1999.

Photographed in the final year of the
millennium, Delaware-Lackawanna
No. 310, a C-420 built by the former
American Locomotive Company in
1964, shows the signs of wear one
would expect to see after 35 years on
the job. But along with the thousands
of locomotives that have gone before
it, it represents the inestimable contri-
bution that railroading has made to
the fabric of this remarkable century.

2000
Amtrak (National Railroad Passenger Corporation) Acela

Bombardier/Alsthom High-Speed
Electric Passenger Trainset

In the year 2000, the promise of
U.S. high-speed rail travel is finally
becoming a reality with Amtrak's
new Acela. Earlier American efforts
to utilize European high-speed developments—including Amtrak's own
1980s experiments with the French
Turboliner and the Canadian LRC—
fizzled out due to the expense of
roadbed improvements.

But in 1999, with necessary track
improvements in place, Amtrak began
converting its Northeast Corridor
"Metroliner" operations to what it
calls "Acela" service (from "accelera-
tion" and "excellence")—spearheaded

by a new high-speed electric train.
The Acela trainset was developed by a
consortium of Canada's Bombardier
and France's Alsthom, builder of the
TGV (see 1979). Like the earlier
LRC, it employs tilt technology to
produce a smooth ride at speeds up
to 150 mph—and will ultimately cut
Washington–New York trip times to
less than three hours. Twenty Acela
trains are scheduled to be in service
by early fall 2000. This one was
photographed during testing in the
summer of 1999.

The Next Century

After a tumultuous century that saw them reach the pinnacle of wealth and power during its first half—then "crash and burn" shortly thereafter—North American railroads of the last few decades have had to rebuild themselves from the ashes of their predecessors and begin looking to the future.

Large freight carriers, often resulting from mergers of smaller lines, are finding new ways to compete with other methods of transporting goods throughout the continent. And now that they are no longer the primary mode of intercity travel, passenger railroads like America's Amtrak and Canada's Via Rail must offer riders new equipment and services in order to hold on to their piece of the pie. All of this means exciting days ahead for those who believe that rail transportation still has a place in the twenty-first-century world—and for railfans both in North America and abroad.

During the past few decades, rail passengers in Europe and Asia have already been enjoying the fruits of innovations in high-speed rail development. Since the late 1970s, France's TGV *(Train à Grande Vitesse)* has been whisking passengers along at speeds above 160 mph. Such European capitals as Paris, Brussels, and Amsterdam are linked by the high-speed Thalys train. In Spain, riders have two systems to choose from: the Talgo (which connects with cities in France, Portugal, Italy, and Switzerland) and the AVE *(Alta Velocidal Española)*. And it's now possible to travel from London to Paris by rail, via the Channel Tunnel aboard the high-speed Eurostar.

Despite its exciting and proven success in Europe, high-speed rail technology hasn't been effectively exploited in North America until now, primarily because the high costs of track and roadbed improvements needed to make existing tracks safe for high-speed operation have scared companies off. Although Via Rail has been operating fast LRC trains utilizing tilt-technology in Canada since the 1980s, Amtrak eventually scrapped plans for significant use of these trains after limited service.

But after investing in track improvements and revisiting high-speed tilt technology with its new Acela trains (designed and built by French and Canadian companies), Amtrak

Built by a consortium of GM/EMD, Talgo, and Pacifica Marine, Amtrak's new Cascades trainsets in the Pacific Northwest (like the Mt. Hood, seen here powered by an F-59-PHI) employ pendular technology to eventually achieve speeds in excess of 125 mph, once track improvements scheduled for the early twenty-first century are completed.

has finally embarked on a project that will bring a true high-speed train—capable of up to 150 mph—into operation on American rails in the year 2000. By the time you read this, the first sleek Acela trains will have entered into service on Amtrak's New York–Washington line.

Perhaps, however, the real future of railroading in the twenty-first century—and beyond—lies in the work currently underway throughout the world by developers of rail systems using magnetic levitation (maglev) technology. Two major projects in Japan and one in Germany have created operational systems based on this exciting technology, which employs electromagnetic power to propel trains along a set of tracks at extremely high speeds, with no actual contact between the tractive equipment and the rails.

Germany's Transrapid project has developed an operational maglev system for future deployment in a planned high-speed service between Berlin and Hamburg beginning sometime after the turn of the century. And two Japanese maglev projects—one already operational, and another in an experimental phase—have yielded remarkable results that point to a bright future for this cutting-edge rail technology.

Currently in service in several Japanese cities, the HSST (High-Speed Surface Transport) system offers three separate approaches to high-speed maglev transport. The HSST-100 urban commuter system is designed for duty within city limits. Running radially through an urban center or in loops around it on overhead tracks, its noiseless,

vibration-free trains can operate without disturbing quiet zones such as hospitals and schools. For suburban commuters, the HSST-200 system runs on rails supported by pillars integrated into the overall track structure, thus avoiding interruption of local traffic below. And the HSST-300, designed for interurban and trunk-line duty, can also be employed for high-speed shuttle service between outlying airports and cities.

And yet another Japanese maglev train—the experimental MLX01 five-car trainset developed by Tokyo's Railway Technology Research Institute—achieved a maximum speed of 552 km/hour (343 mph) in a manned test in April 1999! As these and other projects continue into the year 2000 and beyond, there's no telling how fast trains may be going by the time the twenty-first century turns into the twenty-second.

With fast, new streamlined locomotives like EMD's F-59-PHI (represented here by Amtrak No. 452) leading the way, North America's passenger railroads are attempting to catch up with European developments in high-speed rail as the new century dawns.

Railroad Museums

The following are just a few of many institutions with significant collections of historic locomotives and rolling stock (some of which appear in this book), and other exhibits pertaining to the history of railroading in North America.

Age of Steam Railroad Museum
Fair Park
P.O. Box 15329
Dallas, TX 75315-3259
Tel.: 214-428-0101
www.startext.net/homes/railroad
Email: railroad@arlington.net

B&O Railroad Museum
901 West Pratt Street
Baltimore, MD 21223
Tel.: 410-752-2490
www.borail.org

California State Railroad Museum
111 "I" Street
Sacramento, CA 95814-2265
Tel.: 916-445-7387
       916-445-6645, ext. 7245
          (recorded information)
www.csrmf.org
Email: csrmf@csrmf.org

Canadian Railway Museum
122A Saint-Pierre Street
Saint-Constant, Quebec, Canada
Tel.: 514-632-2410 (information)
       514-638-1522 (administration)
Fax: 514-638-1563
Email: mfcd@quebectel. com

Danbury Railway Museum
120 White Street
Danbury, CT 06813
Tel.: 203-778-8337
Fax: 203-778-1836
www.danbury.org/org/drm

Henry Ford Museum/Greenfield
       Village Railroad
P.O. Box 1970
Dearborn, MI 48121
Tel.: 313-271-1620
www.hfmgv.org/index.html

Illinois Railway Museum
P.O. Box 427
Union, IL 60180
Tel.: 815-923-4391
       815-923-4000 or 800-BIG-RAIL
          (recorded information)
www.irm.org

Museum of Transportation
3015 Barrett Station Road
St. Louis, MO 63122
Tel.: 314-965-7998
Fax: 314-965-0242

National Railroad Museum
2285 South Broadway Street
Green Bay, WI 54304
Tel.: 920-437-7623

Railroad Museum of Pennsylvania
Route 741, P.O. Box 15
Strasburg, PA 17579
Tel.: 717-687-8628
Fax: 717-687-0876
www.rrmuseumpa.org
Email: frm@redrose.net

Orange Empire Railway Museum
P.O. Box 548
2201 South A Street
Perris, CA 92572-0548
Tel.: 909-943-3020
www.oerm.mus.ca.us
Email: info@mail.oerm.org

Smithsonian Institution/Railroad Hall
National Museum of American
       History
14th Street and Constitution Avenue
Washington, DC 20560

Steamtown National Historic Site
150 S. Washington Avenue.
Scranton, PA 18503
Tel.: 717-340-5200

Virginia Museum of Transportation
303 Norfolk Avenue
Roanoke, VA 24016
Tel.: 540-342-5670
Fax: 540-342-6898
www.vmt.org

West Coast Railway Heritage Park
39645 Government Road
Squamish, British Columbia, Canada
Tel.: 604-898-9336
       800-722-1233
Fax: 604-898-9349
www.wcra.org

Selected Operational Historic/Tourist Railroads

The following is a selection of operating tourist railroads allowing riders to experience real rail travel along scenic, historic trackage on vintage steam and/or diesel equipment; some also have large collections of rolling stock on display.

BC Rail, Ltd. (steam)
1311 West First Street
North Vancouver, British Columbia
Canada
Tel.: 604-631-3500 or 800-663-8238
www.bcrail.com

Black Hills Central Railroad (steam)
222 Railroad Avenue
Hill City, SD
Tel.: 605-574-2222
www.1880train.com

Branson Scenic Railway (diesel)
206 East Main Street
Branson, MO
Tel.: 417-334-6110 or 800-2TRAIN2

Cape Cod Railroad (diesel)
252 Main Street
Hyannis, MA
Tel.: 508-771-3788

California Western Railroad/Skunk
        Train (steam, diesel)
Fort Bragg and Willits, CA
Tel.: 800-77-SKUNK or 707-964-6371

Cumbres & Toltec Scenic Railroad
        (steam/narrow gauge)
500 Terrace Avenue
Chama, NM
Tel.: 505-756-2151
        888-CUMBRES

Durango & Silverton Narrow-Gauge
        Railroad (steam/narrow
        gauge)
479 Main Avenue
Durango, CO
Tel.: 888-TRAIN-07

Grand Canyon Railway (steam)
235 North Grand Canyon Boulevard
Williams, AZ
Tel.: 800-THE TRAIN (843-8724)
www.thetrain.com

Kentucky Central Railway (steam)
U.S. 460 East
North Middletown Road
Paris, KY
Tel.: 606-293-0807

Mount Washington Cog Railway
        (steam/narrow gauge)
Route 302
Bretton Woods, NH
Tel.: 800-922-8825
        603-278-5404

Mt. Rainier Scenic Railroad (steam)
Highway 7
Elbe, WA

Tel.: 360-569-2588
New York, Susquehanna & Western
        Railway (steam, diesel)
West Jefferson Street
Syracuse, NY
Tel.: 800-FOR TRAIN (367-8724)
        315-424-1212

Ohio Central Railroad (steam, diesel)
111 Factory Street
Sugarcreek, OH
Tel.: 330-852-4676

Strasburg Railroad (steam)
Route 741
Strasburg, PA
Tel.: 717-687-7522
www.800padutch.com/srr.html

Steamtown National Historic Site
        (steam)
150 South Washington Avenue
Scranton, PA
Tel.: 717-340-5200

Seminole Gulf Railway (diesel)
4410 Centerpointe Drive
Fort Myers, FL
Tel.: 941-275-8487
        800-SEM-GULF
www.semgulf.com

Valley Railroad (steam)
(Essex Steam Train)
Route 154
Essex, CT
Tel.: 860-767-0103
www.valleyrr.com

Waterloo-St. Jacobs Railway (diesel)
10 Father David Bauer Drive
Waterloo, Ontario, Canada
Tel.: 800-754-1054
        519-746-1950

Photo Credits

Acknowledgments

The authors would like to extend their heartfelt thanks to the many people whose generous help made this book possible. First, to the staff members at the various museums we visited, who gave of their time and expertise to assist us in researching and photographing their collections, including: the staff at the Steamtown National Historic Site (Scranton, PA), especially to Ken Ganz, without whose help this book could not have been completed, and others including Superintendent Terry Gess, Assistant Superintendent Kip Hagen, Ralph Courey, Nick Spock of the Reading Technical and Historical Society (PA), and Ken Rigel; the volunteers at Danbury Railway Museum (CT), including Dave Lowry; the various people at the B&O Railroad Museum (MD), especially Courtney B. Wilson, Curator of Collections, Ann Calhoun, Kevin Gillespie, and Abbi Wicklein-Bayne; Kenton Forrest of the Robert W. Richardson Railroad Library at the Colorado Railroad Museum (Golden, CO); Warren Calloway, Bonnie and Dick Corwin, Nick Callas, Ken Rucker, and Ham Sissum at the National Capitol Museum (Wheaton, MD); Paul Hammond and Wally Richards at the Orange Empire Museum (Perris, CA); the staff of the Railroad Museum of Pennsylvania at Strasburg; and the folks at the Strasburg Railroad (PA), the Valley Railroad (Essex, CT), and the Old Colony & Fall River Railroad Museum (MA). Thanks also to Steve Barry and the staff of Railfan Magazine for allowing us to participate in the night photo shoots both at Steamtown and at Danbury, and to Theresa Gren of the Washington State Department of Transportation.

An especially grateful tip of our engineer's cap (and a toot of the whistle) goes to the dedicated railfans/lensmen who graciously allowed us permission to use their photographs: Dave Crosby, Ken Ganz, Jeff Lubchansky, Ed Vebell, and Don Winslow. And finally, a thousand thanks to Sally Anderson, who copyedited, proofread, and otherwise whipped the project into shape in its final stages; to Marilyn Bliss, our indispensable indexer; and to our long-suffering wives, families, colleagues, and friends.

North America's freight railroads will continue to count on high-horsepower diesels - like Burlington Northern-Santa Fe No. 4847, a GE-built Dash 9-44-CW, to haul their cargoes well into the 21st century.

Index

Akron, Canton & Youngstown, 18
Alco (American Locomotive
        Company), 40, 53, 78, 82, 90,
        99, 110, 115, 116, 118–19,
        148, 149, 154
    Brooks Works, 14, 18
    Cooke Works, 16, 43
    Schenectady Works, 30, 119
Alsthom, 131, 156
American Car and Foundry, 21
Amtrak (National Railroad
        Passenger Corporation), 158–59
    Acela, 156–57, 159
    Metroliner, 134–35, 156
    No. 27-28, 102
    No. 417, 112
    No. 700, 150–52
    No. 953, 134–35
ASEA, 134
Atchison, Topeka & Santa Fe
        Railroad, 127
Atlantic City Railroad, 14
Atlantic Coast Line, 14
Auto-Train, 113
AVE (Alta Velocidal Española), 158

Baldwin Locomotive Works, 14, 31,
        32, 36, 46, 51, 54, 65, 87,
        89, 93, 148
    No. 26, 54–57
Baltimore & Ohio Railroad, 68, 73,
        93
    No. 10, 23
    No. 51, 70–71
    No. 633, 100–101
    No. 1961, 110
    No. 3684, 116
    No. 4500, 36
    No. 5300 President Washington,
        54
    No. 7402, 114–15
Berlin Mills Company, 29
Berlin Mills Railway No. 7, 28–29
blower duct, free-flow, 138
B&O Railroad Museum (Baltimore),
        14, 21, 23, 29, 36, 53, 54,
        71, 81, 87, 93, 97, 99, 110,
        115, 116
Bombardier, 156
Boston & Maine Railroad
    No. 314, 129
    No. 3713 The Constitution, 62–63
Bowen, Henry B., 58
Brooks-Scanlon Corporation No. 1,
        32
Budd cars, 102, 110, 144
Budd Company, 110, 134
Bullard Company No. 2, 68–69
Burlington Zephyr, 62
Burnham, Williams & Company, 18

C. W. Blakeslee & Sons, 36
cabs
    all-weather, 43
    box, 23
    camelback, 14
    Mother Hubbard, 14
    tight-clearance, 119

Canadian Government Railways
    No. 2854, 35
    No. 2977, 38
Canadian Locomotive Company, 73
    Kingston Works, 35, 38
Canadian National Railways
    No. 47, 30–31
    No. 3254, 34–35, 38
    No. 3377, 38–39
Canadian Pacific Railway, 146
    No. 1828, 58
    No. 2816, 58–59
    No. 2929, 72–73
    No. 3057, 138–39
    No. 5425, 122–23
Carpenter-O'Brien Lumber Company,
        32
CC&L No. 103, 14
Central Railroad of New Jersey,
        18, 31, 32, 129, 141
    No. 592, 14
    No. 1000, 52–53
Channel Tunnel, 158
Chappell, Gordon, 68
Chesapeake & Ohio Railway
    Huntington Shops, 87
    No. 377, 14–15
    No. 490, 86–87
    No. 1309, 92–93
    No. 1604, 80–81
Chicago Union Transfer Railway No.
        100, 16
Cincinnati, New Orleans & Texas
        Pacific Railway, 32
Colorado Railroad Museum (Golden),
        12
commuter trains, 102–103, 106–107,
        108–109, 112–13, 134, 142,
        144–45, 159. See also
        trolleycars
Compania Azucarera Central Reforma
        No. 8, 40
Connecticut Valley Railroad
        Museum, 113
Consolidated Rail Corporation
        (Conrail)
    No. 1983, 129
    No. 4122, 152–53
    No. 5024, 141
    No. 6042, 142–43
    No. 6151, 146
    No. 6563, 136–37
    No. 6702, 136
    No. 6905, 120–21
    No. 6908, 120–21
    No. 7896, 122
crane idler car, 29
CSXT, 99, 129, 141
    No. 4550, 115

Damascus Railway, 36
Danbury Railway Museum, 90, 100,
        102, 113
Dansville & Mount Morris
        Railroads, 18
Delaware & Hudson Railway
    Gondola No. 8148, 21
    No. 413, 110–11

No. 7418, 124
Delaware, Lackawanna & Western, 32
Delaware-Lackawanna Railroad No.
        310, 154–55
Denver & Rio Grande Railway, 148
Diesel, Rudolph, 53
Duluth, South Shore & Atlantic,
        146
Dumaine, Frederick C., Sr., 100
Durango & Silverton Narrow-Gauge
        Railroad No. 480, 148

E. J. Lavino & Company No. 3, 53
electric trains, 24–27, 107, 131,
        134, 144–45, 156–57
engines
    Baltic-tank, 31
    diesel, 53, 122
    fireless, 40, 73
    saddle-tank, 29, 36, 53, 68
    Shay-type, 21
    turbocharged, 124
Erie Lackawanna, 129, 141
Erie Railroad No. 835, 96
European trains, 22, 24–27,
        130–31, 158–59
Eurostar, 158
excursion lines, 35, 44–49, 89,
        105, 148, 149. See also narrow-
        gauge lines

"Fair of the Iron Horse"
        (Baltimore), 54
Flagler, Henry M., 132
Florida East Coast Railway (FEC)
    No. 434, 140
    No. 445, 132–33
    No. 501, 128–29
    No. 663, 102
"From the Terrace" (film), 89

General Electric Corporation, 23,
        53, 65, 115, 116, 120, 124,
        136, 141, 142, 146, 152
General Motors, Electro-Motive
        Division, 71, 85, 94, 96, 100,
        102, 105, 108, 112, 115, 116,
        122, 124, 127, 129, 132, 134,
        136, 138, 142, 146, 152–53
Gettysburg Railroad, 35
gondola cars, 21
Grand Trunk Railway, 29, 31
Grand Trunk Western Railroad No.
        6039, 50–51
Grazer Waggon Fabrik (GVB) No.
        120, 22
Great Depression, 55, 62, 65
Great Western Railroad, 46
Green Mountain, 90
Greenbrier, Cheat & Elk Railroad
        No. 1, 20–21
Gulf, Mobile & Ohio, 90

H. K. Porter Company, 40, 68
Heisler Locomotive Works, 73
horsepower
    170 units, 100
    300 units, 53

600 units, 100
800 units, 100
900 units, 100
1000 units, 82, 90, 100, 110, 154
1200 units, 100
1500 units, 94, 102, 119, 127,
        149
1600 units, 99, 149
1750 units, 102
1800 units, 148
2000 units, 96, 110, 122, 124,
        129, 138, 154–55
2250 units, 96, 120, 129
2300 units, 120, 124
2400 units, 96, 112
2500 units, 115
2600 units, 112
3000 units, 115, 116, 118, 122,
        124, 129, 132, 134, 136,
        140, 142
3200 units, 152
3300 units, 116
3500 units, 136, 146
3600 units, 116, 141
3800 units, 136, 146
4000 units, 142, 146, 152
7000 units, 134
HSST (High-Speed Surface
        Transport), 159

Illinois Central Gulf, 90
Illinois Central Railroad No. 790,
        16–17, 30
Illinois Terminal, 90
Industrial Works, 29
Ingersoll-Rand, 53

J. G. Brill Company, 62
Jackson Iron and Steel Company, 55
Jacksonville, St. Augustine and
        Halifax River Railway, 132
Japanese trains, 159

Knox & Lincoln, 30

Lackawanna Valley Railroad, No. 901,
        116–17
Leeds & Farmington, 30
Lehigh & Hudson, 129, 141
Lehigh Valley Railroad, 18, 32,
        129, 141
Lima Locomotive Works, 21, 62, 81,
        85
locomotives. See also engines
    AEM-7, 134
    AMD-110 "Genesis," 152
    B-36-7 (Dash-7), 141
    "Big Boy," 74–77, 78–79
    C-30-7 (Dash-7), 136
    C-39-8-E, 142
    C-40-8 (Dash 8-40C), 142
    C-40-8-W, 142, 146
    C-415, 119
    C-420, 110, 154–55
    C-430, 118–19
    CF-7, 127
    Class 70-3, 21
    Class B1, 68

Class CE-1, 23
Class E-7, 85, 96
Class E-8, 96
Class E-9, 96
Class E-9A, 112
Class EA, 71
Class EP20, 85
Class F-1-a, 73
Class F-2-a, 73
Class F-7A, 97
Class FL-9, 108
Class FP-7, 94
Class G-3, 58
Class GG-1, 62, 65, 68
Class H-1-b, 58
Class H-6, 93
Class I-10a, 89
Class K-4, 60
Class L-1, 87
Class M-1, 60, 87
Class P-4-a, 62
Class RS-1, 82, 90, 99
Class RS-2, 99
Class S-1-d, 38
Class S-2, 85
Class T-1, 89
diesel-electric, 70–71, 82, 85,
    90–91, 94–105, 108–29,
    132–43, 146–55
electric, 23, 53, 65, 68, 131,
    134, 156
F-40-PH, 134, 142
F-40-PHL-2, 142
GG-1, 134
GP-7, 102
GP-9, 102, 105
GP-38, 122, 124, 138
GP-38-2, 122, 124, 129, 138
GP-39-2, 124
GP-40, 116, 124, 129, 140
GP-40-2 (Dash-2), 116, 129, 140
GP-40-3, 124
NW-2, 100
P-32-AC-DM, 152
RS-3, 99
RS-10, 148
RS-11, 148
RS-18, 148
RS-18-2, 148
RS-18-R, 148
RS-36, 148
RSC-2, 149
SD-35, 115
SD-40, 115, 136
SD-40-2, 122
SD-50, 136, 146
SD-50-2, 136
SD-60, 136, 146
SD-60-M, 146
SD-60-MAC, 153
SD-70-MAC, 153
SD-80-MAC, 152–53
steam, 12, 14–21, 29–63, 68–69,
    72–81, 84–89, 92–93, 148

SW-1, 100
SW-7, 100
SW-8, 100
SW-900, 100
U-23B, 120, 124, 129
U-23C, 120
U-25B, 115, 116
U-25C, 115
U-30B, 116
Loewy, Raymond, 65
Louisa Railroad, 14
Lowville & Beaver River Railroad
    No. 1923, 40

Mack Company, 100
magnetic levitation (maglev)
    technology, 159
Maine Central Railroad No. 519, 30
    No. 228, 115
Maine Shore Line, 30
Mallet, Anatole, 93
MBTA, 112
McGinnis, Patrick, 102
Metro-North Commuter Railroad
    New Haven Line, 144–45
    No. 2024, 108–109
Middletown & Hummelstown Railroad
    No. 1016, 154
Minneapolis, St. Paul & Sault Ste.
    Marie, 146
Monongehela Connecting Railroad
    No. 701, 119
Montreal Locomotive Works, 31, 58,
    148
Moosehead Line, 30
Morrison-Knudsen, 142

narrow-gauge lines, 12, 24–27, 148
National Capitol Trolley Museum
    (Wheaton), 22
National Railway Museum
    (Montreal), 73
New Haven Railroad No. 15, 100,
    108
New Haven Trap Rock Company
    (Branford Steam Railroad) No.
    43, 36–37
New Hope & Ivyland Railroad No.
    1513, 149
New Jersey Transit No. 4129, 134
New York, Chicago & St. Louis
    Railroad (Nickel Plate Road),
    14
    No. 44, 18–19
    No. 514, 104–105
    No. 757, 84–85
    No. 759, 85
New York, New Haven & Hartford
    Railroad, 144
    No. 140-141 Roger Williams,
    102–103
    No. 0673, 90–91
New York, Susquehanna & Western
    Railway No. 3000, 118–19

New York Central Railroad, 85,
    116, 118–19, 144
    No. 4096, 112–13
New York World's Fair (1939–40),
    73
Nickel Plate Road. See New York,
    Chicago & St. Louis Railroad
Norfolk & Western, 21
    No. 2514, 105
Norfolk Southern Corporation, 105,
    129, 141
Northern Pacific, 89
Norwood & St. Lawrence Railroad
    No. 210, 42–43

Oakland Bay Rapid Transit No. 167,
    107
Oneida & Western Railroad No. 20,
    32
Orange Empire Rail Museum
    (Perris), 107

Penn Central, 119, 129, 141
    No. 83-84, 102
Pennsylvania Power & Light Company
    No. 2, 73
    No. 4094, 73
Pennsylvania Railroad, 14
    Altoona Works, 60, 65, 68
    No. 4800, 64–67
    No. 5690, 68
    No. 5901, 85
    No. 6755, 60–61
Pere Marquette Railway, 14
Philadelphia & Reading Railroad,
    73
    No. 1187, 18
Philadelphia & Western No. 205, 62
Poland Spring Railroad Engine No.
    2, 53
Portland & Kennebec, 30
Public Service Electric & Gas
    Company No. 6816, 40–41
Pullman, George Mortimer, 83
Pullman Company No. 7437, 83

Rahway Valley Railroad No. 15,
    32–33
railbuses, 100
Railroad Control Act, 36
Railroad Museum of Pennsylvania
    (Strasburg), 60, 68, 73, 85,
    119
Railway Technology Research
    Institute (Japan), 159
Reading & Northern Railroad No.
    2399, 124–25
Reading Company, 18
    No. 902, 94–95
    No. 2124, 88–89
Reading Railroad, 129, 141
Remington Arms Company No. 2, 100
Rio Grande Southern Railroad No.
    20, 12

Rock Island Railroad, 90, 115
Rogers Works, 43

Schenectady Works (Schenectady
    Locomotive Engine
    Manufactory), 12, 119. See also
    Under Alco
self-propelled cars, 110
SEPTA, 62
Shay, Ephraim, 21
Siemens Transportation Systems,
    153
sleeping cars, 83
SNCF (French National Railways)
    "Little Yellow Train," 24–27
    TGV, 130–31, 158
Soo Line No. 6059, 146–47
speed, 14, 96, 131, 134, 156,
    158–59
Steamtown National Historic Site
    (Scranton), 16, 18, 29, 30,
    31, 32, 35, 36, 38, 40, 53,
    55, 68, 73, 74–77, 85, 105
Stourbridge Railroad No. 44,
    126–27
Strasburg Railroad Company, 18
    No. 90, 44–49
streamlining, 62, 71, 86–87, 96,
    110, 150–52
switchers
    diesel-electric, 53, 82, 90, 99,
        100, 110, 115, 118, 119,
        127, 129, 141, 142, 148,
        154–55
    electric, 23, 68
    steam, 18, 40, 53, 54–57, 73

Talgo, 158
Thalys, 158
trainsets, 131, 156, 159
trams, 22
Transcontinental Railroad, 78
Transrapid, 159
Tri-Rail No. 805, 142
trolleycars, 22, 62

"U-boats," 115, 116, 120, 124,
    129, 136, 141
Union Pacific Railroad
    No. 912A, 112
    No. 4012, 78–79
United States Railroad
    Administration (USRA), 36, 51
U.S. Army Corps of Engineers No.
    8077, 82

Via Rail, 158
Virginia Central, 14
Vulcan Iron Works, 29, 36

Washington Terminal Company No.
    500-501, 29
Western Maryland Railway
    No. 195, 98–99